WOMEN
&CHURCH
LEADERSHIP

WOMEN
& CHURCH
LEADERSHIP

E. Margaret Howe

ZONDERVAN
PUBLISHING HOUSE   OF THE ZONDERVAN CORPORATION
GRAND RAPIDS, MICHIGAN 49506

WOMEN AND CHURCH LEADERSHIP
Copyright © 1982 by The Zondervan Corporation
Grand Rapids, Michigan

First printing: January 1982

Library of Congress Cataloging in Publication Data
Howe, E. Margaret.
Women and church leadership.

Includes bibliographical references and index.
1. Women clergy. 2. Women in Christianity.
3. Church officers. I. Title.
BV676.H68   262'.14   81-16339
ISBN 0-310-44571-X   AACR2

Unless otherwise indicated,
Scripture quotations are from the Revised Standard Version,
copyright © 1946, 1952
by the Division of Christian Education
of the National Council of Churches of Christ
in the United States of America

Edited by Judith E. Markham and Diane Zimmerman

Printed in the United States of America

To my parents

CONTENTS

ABBREVIATIONS

ACW	*Ancient Christian Writers: The Works of the Fathers in Translation* (Quasten and Plumpe)
ANF	*The Ante-Nicene Fathers* (Roberts and Donaldson)
CD	Cairo Damascus Document
FC	*The Fathers of the Church*
JES	*Journal of Ecumenical Studies*
NCE	*New Catholic Encyclopedia*
NPNF	*Nicene and Post-Nicene Fathers* (Schaff)
TDNT	*Theological Dictionary of the New Testament* (Kittel and Bromiley)

INTRODUCTION

"What is it you women want?" a friend inquired recently. He had heard of my involvement in the discussion concerning the role of women in the church. "The church is a community," he said, "and women are already a part of that community." And as if to settle in advance any further issues which might arise, he hastened to add, "Our calling is to live the Christian life and thus present Christ to the world—no one is holding you women back from doing that."

Significant words. But I was bewildered. Could it be that the demands Christian women are making are so unreasonable, so fantastic, that they cannot be understood by the average member of a church congregation? Are the issues so obscure that they seem trifling and irrelevant? Is the question concerning the role of women in the church simply an irritating conundrum which unnecessarily impedes the effective functioning of the body of Christ?

Certainly it is true that the church is a community of which women form a sizable part. And no one can deny that the reason this community exists is to represent Christ in the midst of the turmoil and complexity of everyday life. Women are not denied this privilege. But there are issues which run much deeper and which demand a sincere and genuine response. It is disconcerting to be forced to reexamine presuppositions which have been held to tenaciously for generations. It is profoundly disturbing to face the possibility that over a long period of time the church may have been denying to women the place assigned to them by God. But there is no growth without pain and struggle, and in this area, as in others, the church must come to maturity.

This present volume represents some small involvement in that pain and struggle. Consideration is given to sensitive issues— issues which concern changing patterns of church leadership and changing attitudes toward women. It cannot be said that the matter has been settled because there are now churches which ordain women as ministers. This situation simply presents a continuing challenge. On the one hand, there is a need to examine the reasons why some Christian communities, including the Roman Catholic church, cannot as yet reconcile themselves to ordaining women. On the other hand, within those churches which do ordain women to ministry, there is an even greater need for congregations to understand what it means for a woman to fulfill a role which has for many centuries been assigned exclusively to men. It is possible that a decision made at the council table of a leading denomination may not be fully understood by the men and women who share membership in that community. Some of those people may have misgivings. Some may not be aware of the underlying principles which have brought about new attitudes and procedures.

Too often in the past lay people have been deprived of the opportunity to consider the process of reasoning that led to certain decisions within the church. There was a time, for example, when the Bible was circulated only in Latin. English-speaking Christians were totally dependent on the clergy for the communication of its message. It was the dream of Erasmus, a great biblical scholar of the sixteenth century C.E., that this state of affairs should be remedied. "Christ desires his mysteries to be published abroad as widely as possible," Erasmus wrote in the preface to his Greek New Testament. "I could wish that even all women should read the Gospel and St. Paul's epistles. . . . I wish that the farm worker might sing parts of them at the plough . . . and that the traveler might beguile the weariness of the way by reciting them."[1] William Tyndale sought to make that dream come true by translating the Bible into English. For his efforts he was put to death, and copies of his English translation of the Bible were seized and destroyed. Church dignitaries feared that lay people might be led astray if allowed such direct access to the holy writings.

Fortunately such times are past. Today lay people of our churches are encouraged to pursue an honest and individual search for truth. The facts are openly available to all and may be considered and assessed. In such a healthy environment of inquiry it is possible to arrive at a balanced understanding of the direction in which the present-day church is being called to move. This volume, *Women and Church Leadership,* brings together careful biblical exegesis of the pertinent texts (chapters 1-3), a study of the writings and practices of the early church (chapters 4-6), and investigation of current policies among various Christian denominations (chapters 7-11). Academic inquiry thus goes hand in hand with exposure to real-life situations in the churches of today.

The preparation of this manuscript was facilitated by the fact that Western Kentucky University granted me a sabbatical leave for the duration of the academic year 1979-1980. I appreciate this very much. I am grateful also to the Institute for Advanced Christian Studies which awarded me a generous grant, enabling me to study for one semester at the Ecumenical Institute for Theological Studies in Jerusalem, Israel. My appreciation extends also to Fuller Theological Seminary, Pasadena, California, for the use of its library facilities and to Dr. Andrée Emery who welcomed me into the fellowship of a Roman Catholic Secular Institute in East Hollywood, where I was able to find much of the material I needed relating to the Roman Catholic tradition.

In addition, my thanks go out warmly to the many women seminarians and women ministers who responded to my questionnaire. Considering their heavy work loads and the discursive nature of the questions, it was almost too much to hope that they would respond. Not only did they do so with enthusiasm, but many of them wrote me letters of encouragement and support which renewed my own interest and commitment. This personal contact was very satisfying to me and made me keenly aware of the living reality of the present debate. My editor, Judith Markham, has sustained the project since its inception. Her constructive ideas and constant cheerfulness have enabled me to ride the rough places and have finally brought the project to its completion. Invaluable also has been the help and support of my typist, Cheryl Takayama.

The reader will find in these pages ideas new and old. It is impossible to write on this subject without being influenced by the writings of others, and I hope that credit has been given where it is due. Perhaps the new levels of inquiry in this present work will serve in turn as a platform from which further significant issues may be addressed.

Notes

[1]Erasmus, "Preface to the Greek New Testament," 1516. See F. F. Bruce, *The History of the Bible in English* (Oxford: Oxford University Press, 1978), p. 29.

WOMEN
&CHURCH
LEADERSHIP

INCONSISTENCIES

IT IS NOT uncommon to encounter dialogue between people who hold differing opinions concerning the place of women in the church community. Some people are persuaded that a woman's role is a secondary role. They believe that Christian women may be actively involved in the everyday running of a church, may devote their time to visiting the sick, their money to worthy projects, and their energies to the effective operation of missionary outreach. But they maintain that the decision-making process of the church should be assigned to men, as well as any teaching ministry which is conducted from the pulpit. Some people view the situation from a different perspective. They believe that Christian women should share with men the decision-making processes and should participate freely in the teaching ministry of the church in addition to the activities mentioned above. There are two factors which have a bearing on this situation, namely scriptural principles and cultural influences.

Scriptural Principles

All those holding the opinions cited above are probably convinced that they are structuring their church community in accordance with the principles of Scripture. This is confusing. How could such a situation arise? Are the biblical documents so unclear that they lend themselves to two opposing interpretations of how the membership of a church community should be organized? In response to this question, it should be noted that it is possible that not every church which claims to be basing its structure and beliefs on the teachings of the Bible is in fact doing so. Occasionally a church may attribute to the Bible ideas which in fact represent a more definite stance than that found in the pages of Scripture.[1]

One example of a way in which a church may take a more definite stance than Scripture warrants is seen in the establishing of leadership roles in the Christian community. The New Testament documents are surprisingly silent on this issue. Although the writer of the Book of Acts describes in detail how Christian communities were founded in Jerusalem, Caesarea, Antioch, Cyprus, Asia Minor, and Greece, he gives little insight into how these communities were organized. "Apostles" and "elders" are mentioned in connection with the Jerusalem church (Acts 15:2). Paul appointed "elders" in the churches he founded (Acts 14:23). There were "prophets" and "teachers" in the church of Antioch (Acts 13:1); and there was an "evangelist" in the church at Caesarea (Acts 21:8). The elders of the church at Ephesus are described as "overseers"; they are to "care for the church of God" and to "be alert" to guard against the inroads of heretical teachers (Acts 20:28, 31). But nowhere in Acts is there a clear description of how a church should be structured. This is true also in the canonical letters which are addressed to first-century churches. Although, for example, the Pastoral Epistles outline the qualifications required of a person aspiring to the office of bishop or deacon, the respective duties of each are not elaborated.

Thus, when a group of Christians sets up an organizational structure, that structure cannot be said to conform to a sacred "blueprint" from the pages of the New Testament. There is no such blueprint. Each group creates a model of leadership which best suits its concept of the nature and function of Christians in community. Each selects both office and title, giving to them content which is meaningful for the successful functioning of the group. An understanding of this point is essential when considering the issue of women in leadership positions in the church.

Another example of a way in which a church may sometimes present a viewpoint more clear-cut than the New Testament documents allow relates more specifically to women participating in public worship. Frequently the subject is opened and closed with nothing more than a quick reference to a passage in 1 Corinthians: "The women should keep silence in the churches. For they are not permitted to speak" (1 Cor. 14:34). This, it is supposed, precludes a woman from occupying the pulpit of a church and therefore, by definition, from being ordained as a minister. However, the passage quoted is but a small part of a somewhat lengthy letter. In the previous section of this letter the writer, Paul, gives detailed advice concerning matters affecting public worship in the church of Corinth. In the midst of this advice, Paul launches into a reasoned argument concerning how both men and women should be attired when praying and prophesying in public gatherings of the Christian community (1 Cor. 11:2–16). It is clear from his specific inclusion of the proper attire of women in these circumstances that in the Pauline communities women were actively participating in leading the congregations in such activities. In this context both praying and prophesying imply vocal participation in community worship; so Paul did permit women to speak in church gatherings. The passage mentioned above, therefore, must refer to some particular situation of which the Corinthian church was acutely aware but of which we, nineteen hundred years later, are ignorant. It cannot be used to prohibit women from exercising certain gifts associated with church leadership.

In applying scriptural principles, a church may not only take a more definite position than is scripturally valid, but it may also err in failing to follow an argument through to its logical conclusion. In this same section of 1 Corinthians, Paul makes a clear statement concerning man and woman: "Man was not made from woman, but woman from man. Neither was man created for woman, but woman for man" (1 Cor. 11:8-9). This has on occasion been used to bolster the theory that woman is inferior to man and should therefore be designated to fulfill a secondary role in the church. It is argued that she was created for man and should assume the supportive role, supplying advice and encouragement but not usurping the honor or dignity of man's superior position. But a careful reading of the 1 Corinthians passage reveals that the writer was somewhat uncomfortable with this position. Although the sentiment might have been a correct representation of one particular aspect of Jewish thought current at the time, it did not seem to the writer to tally with common experience or with the spirit of the gospel. Paul is compelled to add in all honesty: "Nevertheless, in the Lord woman is not independent of man nor man of woman; for as woman was made from man, so man is now born of woman. And all things are from God" (1 Cor. 11:11-12). Interdependence is seen by the writer to be a truer reflection of the purpose of God in the differentiation of the sexes. It is this interdependence, therefore, that should be reflected in church organization.

Thus in the debate over church structure and leadership roles, churches must take care not to claim for their own particular stance more biblical authority than the Scripture presents. Scriptural passages appealed to in the debate must be seen in their total context and must be considered in light of the full reasoning of the biblical writer.

Cultural Influences

Conflicting viewpoints among Christians result not only from faulty interpretation and application of the Scriptures, but also from inaccurate knowledge of the text and lack of acquaintance with cultural issues. The Christian message is not a compendium of clear-cut beliefs and practices which must simply be adopted and carried through as a matter of routine. God chose to reveal himself in the form of a human being who was born into a particular milieu—namely Middle Eastern society—and at a particular point of history—the first century C.E. The life of Jesus communicated his message just as powerfully as his teachings. But to be understood, the life of Jesus must be reflected on and comprehended in the light of the culture in which he lived.

There are significant principles underlying each act of Jesus, but these principles are not always obvious on a casual reading of the text. An example of this is found in the gospel narratives which depict Jesus' attitude toward women. It is commonly assumed that because Jesus chose twelve men to be his inner circle of disciples, he had no place in his entourage for women. Stained-glass windows in churches frequently depict the Twelve in association with Jesus; films of the life of Jesus show him seated in the open countryside teaching this group of men; and Leonardo da Vinci's famous painting of the Last Supper portrays an exclusively male gathering celebrating the Passover meal in the Upper Room. However the Gospels indicate that women did travel with Jesus, many of them—some were married and some were single (Luke 8:1-3). Women were often the recipients of his teaching, both in larger gatherings (Matt. 15:38) and in individual encounters (Luke 10:39; John 4:7-30). And if the Last Supper was indeed the Passover meal, it would be unusual if the gathering did not include women.

Actually, acquaintance with the cultural milieu within which Jesus lived reveals some very surprising truths about his relationships with women. It was not common for a rabbi of the time to include women in his group of followers. Nor was it an accepted custom for women to be singled out as recipients of spiritual teaching. Indeed, it was unusual for any Jewish man to talk to a woman in public. Given the cultural background of first-century Palestine, Jesus showed a remarkable sensitivity to women and their place in society. When confronted by the accusers of a woman guilty of adultery, Jesus refused to assent to the commonly accepted theory that only the woman deserved punishment. He drew public attention to the shame of the male involvement in such acts, and at the same time showed a sympathetic understanding of the woman's plight (John 8:2-11). In the Lukan narrative concerning Mary and

Martha, Jesus is again depicted as moving beyond the culturally accepted norms of his time. He gently rebuked Martha for her busy involvement in the preparation of the meal—a traditional role for a Jewish woman; and he openly commended Mary for her curiosity about spiritual matters and her desire to learn from his teaching—a traditional role for a Jewish man (Luke 10:38-42). The woman with whom Jesus dialogued at the well of Sychar had acquired a good grasp of religious history and showed some acquaintance with theological ideas. Jesus respected this and interacted with her thinking on a level that was not always possible in his encounter with men, as for example in his conversation with Nicodemus (John 4:7-26; 3:1-15).

Incidents such as these provide insight into Jesus' attitude toward women. Perhaps the time was not ripe in first-century Palestine for a woman to be named among the Twelve; perhaps the religious milieu of the synagogue and the established social mores of the Semitic peoples precluded this. But Jesus was quick to recognize the dignity of women; he had respect for their ability to grasp and understand spiritual truths, and he considered them worthy recipients of some of his most profound teaching. According to the Gospels of Matthew and John, even the news of the resurrection of Jesus was communicated first to a woman, and to a woman was entrusted its first proclamation (Matt. 28:1-7; John 20:11-17).

A knowledge of the cultural background of the New Testament writers is also helpful when the canonical letters are being considered. Even those who approach the sacred writings believing that they are the inspired Word of God discover sooner or later that there are passages which reflect a cultural situation different from their own. When this happens, a judgment must be made concerning which aspects of the passage are of abiding significance and which aspects are merely a reflection of social custom.

The opening paragraph of 1 Corinthians 11 provides an example of this. In discussing dress codes appropriate for public worship, Paul instructs that the men should not wear any head covering but that the women should be veiled. This was apparently the customary manner of dress for Jewish people of that time on occasions which called for formal attire. It is interesting to note that among Jewish people today custom requires men to cover their heads during public worship, using either the small skullcap (yarmulke) or the larger prayer shawl (tallith), while women may enter the synagogue without a head covering.

What is the custom today among Christian communities? It is true that in the Western world a man does not wear a hat in a Christian place of worship, but this is a reflection of social convention rather than of religious principle. It is the customary way for a man to show respect. Not too long ago, a man would tip his hat when passing a woman on the street, and he would remove his hat when entering a home. It was natural to show the same respect in a place of worship. But what of women? It used to be customary for a woman to wear a hat on any formal occasion, including public gatherings of the church. To appear without a head covering would have been disrespectful. Now the situation is different. Women seldom wear hats, except for fashion purposes. In most congregations in the Western world it is no longer considered disrespectful for a woman to attend a worship service without a head covering. But either way, practice is geared to social convention rather than religious principle. The biblical text speaks not of a hat but of a veil, and this has never been the customary dress for women in Western branches of the church (excepting certain religious orders).[2]

Thus, whether consciously or unconsciously, Christian communities make allowance for the fact that some issues in the Bible are a matter of social convention pertaining to a certain time and to a specific geographical location, sometimes even to a particular ethnic group. To recognize this is not to undermine the message of the Bible, but rather to enhance it. God has ordained that the mind must interact with the scriptural message if it is to become meaningful in every age. Christians must make such judgments in assessing biblical guidelines for Christian living.

Some Christians reject the concept of cultural adaptation. They argue that the church of today should model itself as closely as possible on "the New Testament church" and transcend any cultural differences. Such a proposition is weighted with problems. In the first place, as has been noted above, there is no blueprint for "the New Testament church." The New Testament itself reveals traces of many church communities, each structured to meet the demands of a local situation. Insights gained from the texts are usually matters of general principle which must then be adapted to a given community.

In the second place, the very nature of the gospel demands that it be made relevant to people living at any particular time and in any particular society. It is inevitable, then, that the time and the society will influence the form Christian worship takes. This is healthy and natural. It would be unhealthy and unnatural to perpetuate, as though they were part of the essential core of the Christian faith, practices which are in fact simply one way of giving expression to that faith. To do so would inhibit the impact of the gospel rather than enhance it. It is possible for the church to hold on too long to outmoded forms of worship and thereby fail to be a vehicle through which God can speak to the world today.

Just as inconsistencies may be found in the interpretation and application of scriptural principles, so they may be found in the adoption of certain customary practices that do not necessarily have biblical backing. A church may strongly resist acknowledging that cultural adaptation is necessary and yet allow cultural norms to govern its thinking in relation to women and church leadership. This can be seen when considering the church assembled for worship.

In many churches (although the situation is changing) the person occupying the pulpit is a man. He is responsible for overseeing the worship service. He reads the passages of Scripture assigned for the particular Sunday, and in his sermon he directs the thought of the congregation to matters arising from this Scripture. His message may be geared to teaching Christian doctrine or to explaining Christian ethics. He aims to move his congregation to response, a response that may take the form of repentance, reevaluation of standards and lifestyle, or renewed consciousness of the vitality of the Christian experience. The congregation depends on him for guidance in spiritual matters, for encouragement in times of difficulty, for inspiration when faith is waning.

This is a position of honor within the Christian community. The person so designated becomes the recipient of various tokens of esteem. He bears a title which in some way shows respect for his office, whether it be "Father," "Reverend," "Pastor," or simply "Preacher." He is paid a salary for his services, a salary which usually exceeds that of any other functionary in the local church. He may be provided with a furnished house, and the church will often assume responsibility for the upkeep of the property and grounds, for utility bills, and for transportation. Sometimes he is given an allowance for the purchase of books needed for personal study and for other items. When the church is assembled for worship, this honor is demonstrated visibly by assigning to the leader a seat at the front of the church in clear view of the congregation. He may enter the church from a special door, sometimes in procession, to heighten the sense of honor.

Why this demonstration of respect? Because in showing deference to its leader, the congregation is indirectly demonstrating its respect for the church as an institution. The church is the body of Christ; Christ is the head of the church; the church is the congregation of God. This deferential treatment of church leaders symbolizes respect for God.

But why has this particular leadership position traditionally been assigned to a man? Responses to this question have generally been couched in religious terms, and these are discussed in detail later. Some maintain that the minister is a priest and that the ancient Hebrew priesthood was reserved for men. Some conceive of God as a male being and think it fitting that his representative be male also. Some argue that because the apostles were men, all church ministers should be men.

But is it possible that the underlying reason for the delegation of this position to men is in fact one of cultural adaptation? In Western society for many years the professional opportunities open to men have far exceeded those open to women, particularly in those considered leadership positions. In the medical profession, for example, men were trained as doctors, women as nurses. In the legal sphere, men occupied the positions of attorney, prosecutor, and judge, while women served as legal secretaries. In banking, men were usually found on the board of trustees, making decisions and directing policies; women were the cashiers meeting and serving the public in the day-to-day transactions of the bank. Only in comparatively recent times have women been encouraged to train for the leadership responsibilities. Even today it takes courage and inner strength to do so.

A similar assignment of roles is found in the church. While the leading position has been traditionally reserved for a man, women have been encouraged to work, and to work hard, in lesser spheres. The church secretary is usually a woman. She bears no distinctive title, earns less pay than the minister, and is afforded little prestige. Her duties are performed behind the scenes, mostly out of sight of the congregation. She answers the telephone, keeps up with church records, and generally assists the minister by keeping tabs on his appointments. In many churches women are assigned to the position of Sunday school teacher. This role requires a good acquaintance with biblical studies, an aptitude for coping with the taxing demands of children and adolescents, and a generous allocation of time both in preparation and in performance; but it generally carries no title of honor, no salary, and little recognition.

There are other ways in which the role of women within the church apparently coincides more with culturally conditioned factors than with biblical principles. Western culture has designated a woman's role as the care of children, the preparation of food, and the creation of a pleasing living environment. The church, too, frequently assigns responsibilities in these areas to women. Women care for the church cradle roll and nursery facilities. They organize vacation Bible schools with all manner of craft programs. When sports programs are called for, however, men supervise. Women are responsible for church luncheons, dinners, and receptions and for the provision of food for those in need, even though the indication of Acts 6:2–3 is that Peter appointed seven men to attend to such activities. While the architectural design of the church building usually is the work of men, women are called on to assist in the choice of fabrics and furnishings.

There are problems, too, in attitudes toward sexuality. Although this opinion is not often stated, some people feel it is "improper" for a woman to stand before a church congregation. What is usually implied by this is that a woman's body is sexually stimulating to men and that a church setting is not a suitable place for such stimulation. This also shows how closely so-called religious attitudes are attuned to cultural mores—in this case those of a pagan culture. It is now generally recognized that a man's body can be as attractive to a woman as that of a woman to a man. If either sex finds the human form so preoccupying that it becomes a distraction from worship, the problem lies within that person rather than in the circumstance. Of course, it is possible for a woman or a man to dress seductively, and this would be quite improper in a church setting.

Are women to be held accountable forever for men's passions, while it is discreetly overlooked that men may arouse the same in women? Would it not be more beneficial to encourage wholesome attitudes toward both male and female sexuality by demonstrating in a church setting the ideal way in which a man and woman should present themselves in the presence of God and in the presence of the worshiping congregation? According to Genesis 1:27, the image of God was expressed in the creation of human beings as "male and female." Human sexuality was not viewed as an embarrassment but rather as a reflection in some mysterious way of the very being of God. How appropriate, then, that such an image should be portrayed in the leadership of the church, with both a man and a woman being accorded a leadership role.

Another inconsistency arising from this setting is that although a woman may be barred from the pulpit of some churches on the ground that it is not "proper" for a woman to present herself in public view, it is common practice for these same churches to invite women to participate in choral events and to sing as soloists. Often vocalists dress in gowns that are modest yet feminine, and usually they stand at the front of the auditorium more openly on view than the minister in his pulpit. Yet this is acceptable. Is there some difference between this activity and the delivery of a sermon? Some would argue on the basis of 1 Timothy 2:12, where the writer says, "I do not permit a woman to teach" (NIV), that the issue is really one of content. The soloist is merely singing. She is not instructing the congregation. But Ephesians 5:18–19 indicates that such songs are a medium through which the Holy Spirit is active and that we are to be "addressing one another in psalms and hymns and spiritual songs" because they lead us toward spiritual maturity. A perusal of the words of many of the classic hymns of the church will confirm this sentiment. They are rich in doctrinal content, and some are written to convict and convert the hearers. What right has the church to value one spiritual gift above another? The vocalist is communicating the Word of God to the congregation as surely as is the preacher.

The influence of cultural conditioning is evidenced also in churches founded in developing countries. The history of Christian missions demonstrates that Christian communities which would never permit a woman to assume a leadership role as minister of a local congregation in the homeland apparently have no misgivings about allowing her to assume such a position in a church overseas. Women venture into areas of extreme danger and face enormous hazards in bringing the message of Christ to people who otherwise would not hear or understand it. These women are filling the roles of apostle, evangelist, and teacher. They serve in an ancient tradition of Christian ministry, but they do not receive from the church the recognition of a title, and they work in the face of much financial insecurity. Once their churches become established and stable, and at least partially self-supporting, a man is installed as minister. Does this represent an application of biblical guidelines? Is it not rather the same exploitation as that found in secular culture? Women are assigned to difficult tasks which bring small financial remuneration and little esteem, while men are honored with leadership positions, titles, and financial security.

The matter of cultural adaptation is a delicate issue. On the one hand, the church is required to make the gospel relevant by expressing it in ways which are acceptable in our own cultural environment but which may not necessarily be those which sufficed for first-century Middle Eastern Christian communities. On the other hand, the church is warned against the perils of allowing the cultural norms of contemporary society to dictate the form of its structure and witness. Is it possible to avoid falling between the Scylla and Charybdis of this treacherous sea?

In reality, the course is not as hazardous as it might seem. An awareness of the potential dangers is in itself a safeguard. Within the pages of Scripture are certain clearly defined principles. The task of the church is to understand these and to give expression to them within the context of its own cultural environment. But the scriptural principles themselves must assume priority and must always be the overriding factor. Attention is therefore directed to these in the next three chapters.

Notes

[1]See E. Margaret Howe, "The Positive Case for the Ordination of Women," *Perspectives on Evangelical Theology*, Kenneth S. Kantzer and Stanley N. Gundry, eds. (Grand Rapids: Baker, 1979), pp. 267-76.

[2]For several centuries Spanish women have used the mantilla.

PROBLEMS OF TRANSLATION
AND INTERPRETATION

THERE ARE TWO areas of study which throw considerable light on the leadership functions of women in the context of the church. First, there is the New Testament itself, with its rich variety of documents. Second, there is the broad scope of history—a lengthy time period from the first century to the twentieth century during which the church has struggled to maintain its identity and authenticity. Both of these areas are significant, but each must be approached with caution, for reasons which will be explored in this chapter.

Hazards Along the Way

Those who have taught in a church context know the dismay of turning to a familiar passage of Scripture in order to substantiate a statement, only to find that this particular Bible has it worded differently. Where does one turn from there? The average church member is usually at the mercy of a wide spectrum of Bible translations and has no frame of reference by which to judge which is the most correct. The temptation then arises to select that translation which in most cases seems to agree with what one has always felt to be the truth of a matter. But one's concept of the truth of a matter might well have been formed through habitual use of a rather poor translation. All English translations of the Bible have this in common: they were made at a particular time and by a particular group of people. Both the time and the people are significant factors. Generally speaking, a good translation will be one produced in comparatively recent times because scholars now have access to much earlier and more accurate Greek and Hebrew texts. It will be a translation produced by a group of scholars holding to standards of academic integrity. An individual translator may sometimes communicate his own slant of meaning rather than the intent of the original author. A translation made by a panel of scholars representing one particular denomination within the Christian faith may suffer from similar problems. Fortunately, many excellent Bible translations are available today, produced by groups of scholars representing a variety of religious viewpoints. Even so, no one of these is, or claims to be, a perfect representation of the original texts.

Unfortunately, some translations of the Bible can be misleading for study of the issue of women and church leadership. In the past, Bible translation has been carried out almost exclusively by men. Occasionally the translator's preconceived ideas about the role of women have mitigated against his better judgment in the translation process. Reference works and commentaries reflect a similar weakness. It is important to be aware of this. For the purpose of illustration, three significant passages will be examined: Romans 16:1; Romans 16:7; and 1 Timothy 3:11.

Romans 16:1. Heading the list of people commended by Paul at the end of his letter to the church in Rome is a woman named Phoebe. The Greek text describes her as "deacon *(diakonos)* of the church of Cenchreae." Cenchreae was a port city east of Corinth, situated in an area where Paul himself ministered for several years. Evidently Phoebe was about to visit the church in Rome. Perhaps she was the bearer of this particular letter. This piece of information appears simple enough until one examines the various translations.

The King James Version (1611) overlooks the fact that Phoebe is characterized as holding an ecclesiastical office and describes her as "a servant of the church which is at Cenchrea." Elsewhere when the word *diakonos* occurs in the Greek text, the KJV usually renders it in English as "minister." Timothy, for example, in 1 Timothy 4:6, is described as "a good minister"; Epaphras, in Colossians 1:7, is commended as "a faithful minister of Christ"; Tychicus, in Ephesians 6:21, is called "a faithful minister" (also in Col. 4:7); Paul, in Colossians 1:25, is designated as "minister"; and Paul and Apollos, in 1 Corinthians 3:5, bear the same title, "minister."[1] These people are all men. Why, when a woman's name appeared in the text, did the translators choose to render the word as "servant"? There is a Greek word for servant *(doulos),* but it is not the word in use here. It is true that in secular usage the word *diakonos* referred to one who waited at table, but in the context of the New Testament it usually has reference to a particular church office. There is no objective reason why the word when used of a woman would bear the secular meaning, but when used of a man would bear the religious connotation.

The Revised Standard Version (1952) appears to correct this error. Here Phoebe is described as "a deaconess of the church at Cenchreae." The word most closely corresponding to the Greek *diakonos* is used. The feminine form of the word was not in use at the time, so it would actually have been more correct to have given Phoebe the title of "deacon," but at least the RSV enables the reader to determine her ecclesiastical office. However, a perplexing problem remains. When the same Greek word is used of Timothy, of Epaphras, of Tychicus, and of Paul (in 1 Tim. 4:6; Col. 1:7; Eph. 6:21; and Col. 1:25), the RSV translators chose to use the English word "minister" as the counterpart.

The word "minister" implies service and is quite justifiable as a translation of the Greek *diakonos.* Had the translators also used the word "minister" in their rendering of Romans 16:1, no query would be raised. But the translators of the RSV have left the impression that Phoebe's office was in some way different from that of her male colleagues. And because in the contemporary church setting the title "minister" is more prestigious than that of "deacon,"

Phoebe is placed a little lower on the scale of values than is actually warranted by the text.

When consulting contemporary paraphrases of the Bible, one has cause to be extremely wary. In his *Living Bible,* Kenneth Taylor describes Phoebe as "a dear Christian woman from the town of Cenchreae"! This, of course, bears no relation to the Greek text. When the same Greek expression is found in 1 Timothy 4:6, but with reference to a man, Taylor paraphrases the office as that of "a worthy pastor." Clearly the prejudices of the scholar have had sway here.

What light is thrown on this issue by commentators? In his *Commentary on Romans* Calvin described Phoebe as "an assistant of the Cenchrean church." In his editorial comments John Owen, the translator of the commentary, acknowledges that the Greek text reads *diakonos* and concedes that there is some evidence that women held the office of deacon in the early church. He notes that such an office was instituted "to baptize women, to teach female catechumens, to visit the sick, and to perform other inferior offices in the church." However, Owen goes on to assert that "this was a state of things after the apostolic times, and there is no reason to believe that Phoebe was of this order." He assumes on the basis of Romans 16:2 that Phoebe was "a woman carrying on some business traffic and that she went to Rome partly at least on this account."[2]

In 1880, Frederick Godet, while supporting the probability that women deacons were a feature of the primitive church, wrote, "Why should not a rich and devoted woman . . . have borne, even without ecclesiastical consecration, the title of deaconess?"[3] A more modern commentary, *The Interpreter's Bible,* is also skeptical about the use of the word "deaconess" in Romans 16:1. Although the commentator, John Knox, is well-aware that deaconesses feature in the literature of the early second century C.E., he feels sure they were not recognized in the Pauline churches. The fact that "there is no other allusion to a deaconess in the N.T." seems to confirm him in this opinion.[4] William Plumer, commenting on this passage, writes, "Some have attempted to show that [Phoebe] held the office of deaconess. This can hardly be proven."[5] And H. W. Beyer, commenting on Paul's use of the word *diakonos* in this particular instance, states, "It is, of course, an open question whether [Paul] is referring to a fixed office or simply to [Phoebe's] services on behalf of the community."[6]

A number of assumptions are being made by these commentators, assumptions unjustified by the text. First, it is assumed that a woman deacon would be involved only with ministrations to other women and to the sick. In communities where there were rigid taboos on the intermingling of the sexes, this might well have been practical. But Paul explicitly includes himself among those to whom Phoebe ministered. And he indicates that her business in Rome involves some specific matters affecting the church as a whole and instructs the church to cooperate with her.

Second, it is assumed that Phoebe was a rich woman. That idea is derived from the use of the word *prostatis* in Romans 16:2. This word may be translated "patron" and often had reference to a wealthy benefactor or benefactress. However, the word was used in pagan sources to describe an office bearer in a religious association, or, in the secular world, an individual who acted as legal adviser to people classified as aliens and to slaves who had achieved their freedom. Of course, the more general meaning of "helper" need not be excluded and may in fact be the more realistic one here. The idea of a woman patron, however, seems for some reason to be more acceptable in ecclesiastical circles. If the woman was rich, then she could certainly have been given honor and even a title, but this did not necessarily invest her with any spiritual authority! Godet's comment, "even without ecclesiastical consecration," is an attempt to assure the reader that this was almost certainly withheld. But the text of Romans does not give grounds for such an assumption.

Third, the assumption that there is no other reference to women deacons in the New Testament is open to question in the light of 1 Timothy 3:11. However, even if this were true, would that be adequate grounds for denying that women held such office in the early church? How many times must a concept be featured in the New Testament documents for it to be recognized as a "truth"? Plumer's comment that it can "hardly be proven" that Phoebe was a deacon is equally curious. Why would "proof" be necessary? No such proof is necessary in the case of Epaphras or Tychicus. Why in the case of Phoebe? So also with reference to Beyer's comment: it is not assumed to be "an open question" whether *diakonos* refers to a fixed office when the word describes the activity of a man. Why does it suddenly become "an open question" when a woman is being so designated?

What does emerge from this passage is that a woman was named as a minister of the church of Cenchreae and that she was much respected. In all probability she was the bearer of Paul's letter to the church in Rome, which would account for the positioning of the lofty commendation of her in this passage. This was no small honor and may in itself suggest that she bore official title in the church. Often the bearer of a letter was entrusted also with verbal messages of import which were to be communicated in a more personal way. In addition, Phoebe had in mind some concerns of her own which necessitated the cooperation of the members of the Roman church. Paul evidently felt her concerns worthy of his approbation, for he exhorted this church to give her the support she needed.

Romans 16:7. This same chapter in Romans provides another intriguing insight into the practices of Bible translators. Included in a somewhat lengthy list of greetings are the names "Andronicus and Junias." The RSV reads, "Greet Andronicus and Junias, my kinsmen and my fellow prisoners; they are men of note among the apostles." This gives the clear impression that both were men. Andronicus is certainly a man's name, but there is some ambiguity concerning the name Junias. There are two possibilities: (1) The name is Junias, a contraction of the masculine name Junianus.

(2) The name is Junia, a feminine name common among Roman women. In the Greek language, both names would appear identical, but the contraction of the name from Junianus to Junias is the less common phenomenon; in fact, it is extremely rare if not unknown. Thus, on linguistic grounds it is more likely that Andronicus and Junias were a man and a woman. Interestingly, the KJV even represents the second name as Junia (feminine). However, most of the major Bible translations present the verse as though it had reference to two men. Andronicus and Junias are described as "my kinsmen" and as "men of note among the apostles" rather than as "my relatives" or as "persons of note among the apostles." Why is this?

The key to the situation is to be found in the fact that apostles are mentioned in this context. Some question has been raised concerning whether the phrase "of note among the apostles" implies that these two people were numbered among the apostles and were indeed outstanding apostles, or whether they were people specially singled out for commendation by the apostolic body. The latter interpretation is generally rejected on the basis that the Greek construction hardly bears such a rendering. Andronicus and Junias are therefore designated as apostles and as very significant apostles.

It is well-known that the apostolic body was not restricted to the Twelve. What is not so acceptable to some people is the possibility that a woman might have been designated as "apostle." Commentators have gone to interesting lengths to deny this possibility. Godet assumes that if the name is Junia and refers to a woman, she must have been the sister or wife of Andronicus.[7] Other commentators make a similar assumption. It is true that Prisca and Aquila mentioned in Romans 16:3 were husband and wife, but it by no means follows that when a man and woman were mentioned together they were husband and wife. However, even if Andronicus and Junia were husband and wife, the implication is still that both were apostles.

Because of this clear implication, Godet tends toward the

opinion that the name Junias was the name of a man. Similarly, William Sanday and A. C. Headlam conclude, "If, as is probable, Andronicus and Junias are included among the Apostles, then it is more probable that the name is masculine."[8] The same line of reasoning is followed by William Arndt and F. W. Gingrich who write, "The possibility, from a purely lexical point of view, that this is a woman's name, Junia, is probably ruled out by the context."[9] In other words, although linguistically it is more probable that the reference is to a woman, the fact that it seems to some people unlikely that a woman was numbered among the apostles leads them to translate the name as though it were that of a man.

It is interesting to note that among the patristic writers there were fewer qualms about acknowledging the possibility that a woman could fulfill the office of apostle. John Chrysostom, who was appointed patriarch of Constantinople in 398 C.E., wrote a number of homilies on the biblical texts. In his exposition of Romans 16:7 (Homily 31), Chrysostom comments:

> Indeed to be apostles at all is a great thing. But to be even amongst these of note, just consider what a great encomium this is! But they were of note owing to their works, to their achievements. Oh! how great is the devotion of this woman, that she should be even counted worthy of the appellation of apostle![10]

It is hard to know how to reconcile this with other of Chrysostom's opinions about women. Commenting on 1 Corinthians 14:34–35 (Homily 37), he writes: "The woman is in some sort a weaker being and easily carried away and light minded."[11] Presumably he considered Junia to be an exception to the general rule.

1 Timothy 3:11. This verse provides us with another example of misleading Bible translation. In the context, the author is outlining the qualities required of those appointed to the offices of bishop and deacon. The reader using the KJV will observe that in 1 Timothy 3:11 certain qualities are required of the wives of deacons. "Even so must their wives be grave, not slanderers, sober, faithful in all things." Is this what the author intended? The original text reads, "The women likewise, must be serious . . . ," and this is the translation featured in the RSV.

It is true that the word *woman* in Greek is sometimes used to designate *wife;* but if the author had so intended, then it would have been more natural for him to have introduced a possessive pronoun—and there is no such pronoun in the Greek text (which is why "their" is printed in italics in the KJV). Moreover, the syntax of the passage indicates that the writer intended to direct attention to two distinct groups of people, both falling into a category similar to that of bishop. Verse 8 begins "deacons likewise"; verse 11 begins "women likewise."

If Paul meant to refer to women deacons, why was he not more specific? The answer to this question is that no feminine form of the word *diakonos* was in use at this early time. It would be natural, therefore, for Paul to single out this group by referring specifically to those deacons who were women. A comparison of verses 8 and 11 shows that the qualities required of the men and the women are almost identical. One might assume, therefore, that the instructions included in verse 12 should also be considered applicable to women deacons, namely, that they should be selected from the ranks of women who are faithful to one husband (cf. 1 Tim. 5:9). This is not explicitly stated, but neither is it explicitly stated that a woman deacon should be unmarried.

Thus, in addition to the mention in Romans 16:1 of a woman minister of the church of Cenchreae, Romans 16:7 introduces the possibility that a woman was recognized as an apostle, and 1 Timothy 3:11 strongly indicates that women were appointed as deacons. Unhappily, this information has been obscured in some translations of the Bible.

Elusive Historical Data

The leadership roles assumed by women in the church have been obscured not only in some translations of the Bible but also in various historical records. In 1973 Joan Morris, a British scholar, published a fascinating study entitled *Against Nature and God* (the American edition bears the title *The Lady Was a Bishop*). "History may be hidden in many ways," Morris writes. Sometimes this is due to "evasion of facts through prejudice," and sometimes it is due to "a purposeful malicious hiding of events."[12] Morris illustrated this by showing how the practice of appointing women overseers of churches, a common practice from apostolic times onward for many centuries, was slowly suppressed. In some cases attempts were even made to obscure the records which witnessed to their work.

Morris records, for example, that in the church of Saint Praxedis in Rome there is a mosaic dating from the fifth century C.E. or earlier. It depicts the head of a veiled woman over which is inscribed the title *episcopa* (overseer, bishop). Written vertically alongside is the name Theodo(ra). The last two letters, which represent the feminine form of the name, have been removed from the mosaic and cubes from a later period have been inserted. Similarly, in the catacombs of Priscilla in Via Salerio Nova in Rome there is a fresco depicting a group of women conducting a eucharistic banquet at a funeral service. The figure to the left is apparently the chief celebrant. The head has been sandpapered down to obscure the feminine hairstyle, though the length of the dress clearly indicates to historians that this figure represents a woman. These stone and mosaic inscriptions show that "women once held a place in the hierarchical service of the church that is now denied to them."[13]

Through careful research Morris uncovered evidence which demonstrates that for many centuries women were active in the leadership of churches and of religious communities comprised of both men and women. In fourth century C.E. Asia Minor, for example, a deaconess named Marthana served within a community of men and women which grew up in Seleucia around the shrine of Saint Thecla. The document containing an eyewitness account of this community has been translated and annotated by John Wilkinson, of the British School of Archaeology in Jerusalem, under the title *Egeria's Travels*. Egeria writes:

Round the holy church there is a tremendous number of cells for men and women. And that was where I found one of my dearest friends, a holy deaconess called Marthana. I had come to know her in Jerusalem when she was up there on pilgrimage. She was the superior of some cells of apotactites or virgins. . . . I stayed there, visiting all the holy monks and apotactites, the men as well as the women.[14]

Morris shows how the presence of ordained women in leadership positions was a common phenomenon in both the Eastern and Western branches of the church. As "canonesses," women celebrated the divine office, taught in schools, cared for the sick, and baptized catechumens. As "abbesses," women ruled over communities comprised of both sexes. Although these women did not enjoy the sacerdotal powers of bishops, they fulfilled the duties of bishops in respect to ecclesiastical and civil administration. Many of them were exempt from the authority of a bishop and were directly dependent on the Holy See.

Even though as late as the eighteenth century women were still accepted in leadership positions in the church in England, France, Germany, Italy, and Spain, the history of their involvement has been treated lightly. Morris comments, "The Christian tradition is presented as an all-male right of authority as though it had been so always."[15] For example, many people today would be surprised to learn that the Basilian Order was founded not by Saint Basil but by his sister, Macrina. It is not generally known that Saint Basil in fact lived a monastic life under her guidance. Frequently today the issue of women and church leadership is approached as though women are for the first time in history seeking the right to be appointed to leadership positions. Nothing could be further from the truth. Women are simply seeking to reestablish their claim to leadership positions which were clearly theirs in the early centuries of the Christian Era. These positions were wrested from them by circumstances which do not necessarily bear the mark of divine approval.

What were the factors which brought about a change in the

role of women? Morris suggests that the rise of monasticism and the introduction of the rule of celibacy for priests were influential factors. Rather than being permitted to continue their ministry in parishes and cathedrals, women were cloistered and confined to private chapels. In this way they would not be a source of temptation to male ecclesiastics. In this way also their influence would be curtailed. Another factor is that the concept of "ruling" had become paganized, as evidenced by the fact that by the twelfth century questions were being raised concerning a woman's right to rule over a mixed community. No longer was Christian leadership seen as humble service. Instead, it was regarded as the right of dominion, providing an opportunity for Christians to lord it over one another. Within such an atmosphere as this, male dominance was asserted.

In the debate concerning the leadership of women in the early church, another important factor to consider is that Christian communities evolved from groups of Jews who were regular participants in synagogue worship. The form of synagogue worship influenced the form of Christian worship significantly. It is therefore sometimes thought that the low profile required of women in the context of the Jewish synagogue accounts for the fact that they were denied leadership positions in the church. Women were not appointed as leaders in the synagogues, it is maintained; in fact, they were segregated from Jewish men and took very little part in the public worship patterns of Judaism.

This point of view is open to question. Significant research on the leadership functions performed by women in the ancient Jewish synagogue is being carried out by an American scholar, Bernadette Brooten. In the preparation of her doctoral thesis,[16] Brooten is investigating Greek and Latin inscriptions (contained in Jean-Baptiste Frey, *Corpus Inscriptionum Iudaicarum*) in which women bear such titles as *archisynagogos* (ruler of the synagogue), *presbytera* (elder), *mater synagogae* (mother of the synagogue), and *(h)ierissa* (priestess). In the past, scholars have assumed that because these titles were held by women they must be honorific, perhaps as an extension of a husband's role. Brooten disputes this point of view and assembles evidence to show that women took a much more active part in the ancient Jewish synagogue worship than that which is generally assigned to them by tradition.

As a result of her investigations concerning the function of the ruler of the synagogue, Brooten concludes that this official was a person learned in the Jewish law and was the spiritual director of the congregation. The *archisynagogos* shared with others the responsibility for the collection of money from the congregation and for the erection of new synagogues and the restoration of old ones. The religious and civic functions of the synagogue ruler were not sharply distinguished. In all probability this official functioned not only as a leader of the congregation within the Jewish community but also as a representative of the congregation in the wider context of non-Jewish neighbors and of Roman authorities.

In three of the inscriptions investigated, women synagogue rulers are named without reference to a husband. In several other inscriptions, each of which names a man as *archisynagogos*, the wive's names are mentioned but these women do not bear the title of their husbands. Those scholars who maintain that these titles may be explained away because a woman could not hold such exalted office in the Jewish synagogue are not permitting the evidence to speak for itself. Rather, this evidence supplies traces of a Judaism about which, for lack of sources, we know very little. It is not, for that reason, to be dismissed as inauthentic.

In assessing the influence of Jewish thought on Christian attitudes toward women, caution is necessary. Sometimes the scholar has to admit that there is insufficient evidence from the early centuries to communicate a clear picture of Jewish attitudes toward women in the period which gave birth to the Christian faith. Sometimes, unhappily, the investigator is confronted with evidence that has been influenced by the preconceived ideas of a writer to the detriment of the women concerned.

It is clear that the issues are not as simple as they might appear at first sight. The Bible handled by most churchgoers today is a translation, and caution should be used by those who are not able to consult the original text. Inadvertently or otherwise, translators may sometimes have included readings which are not quite fair to women. Influential commentators have for over a hundred years perpetuated misconceptions in this area of thought, as indeed in some other areas. Discernment is needed when commentaries are consulted. Even historical data is liable to have been colored by prejudice. Scholars of today are endeavoring to uncover these problems and to provide a basis for a more equitable appraisal of the issues.

Notes

[1]Even the agents *(diakonoi)* of Satan mentioned in 2 Corinthians 11:15 are given the title of "ministers" in the KJV. Presumably the translators assumed they were all men!

[2]John Calvin, *Commentary on Romans,* trans. John Owen (Grand Rapids: Eerdmans, 1948), pp. 542–43.

[3]Frederick Godet, *Commentary on Romans,* trans. A. Cusin (Grand Rapids: Zondervan, 1956), p. 488.

[4] *The Interpreter's Bible,* ed. George Arthur Buttrick (Nashville: Abingdon, 1954), 9:655.

[5]William S. Plumer, *Commentary on Romans* (Edinburg: Oliphant, n.d.), p. 638.

[6]H. W. Beyer, in *TWNT,* 2:93.

[7]Godet, *Commentary on Romans,* p. 491.

[8]William Sanday and A. H. Headlam, ICC, *Epistle to the Romans,* p. 423.

[9]William Arndt and F. W. Gingrich, *Greek-English Lexicon of the New Testament,* s.v. *Iounias,* 1st ed. (Chicago: University of Chicago Press, 1979), p. 380. For a more detailed consideration, see Bernadette Brooten, "Junia . . . Outstanding Among the Apostles" (Romans 16:7), *Women Priests: A Catholic Commentary on the Vatican Declaration,* ed. L. Swidler and A. Swidler, (New York: Paulist Press, 1977), pp. 141–44.

[10]In a footnote, the nineteenth-century editor has written, "That a woman should have been an apostle is out of the question"! NPNF, 11:555, n.2.

[11]NPNF, 12:222.

[12]Joan Morris, *Against Nature and God* (London and Oxford: Mowbrays, 1973); Am. Ed., *The Lady Was a Bishop* (New York: Macmillan, 1973), p.xi. (Morris's work has received mixed reviews. See *Expository Times* 86 (October 1974) :30 and *Dialog* 13 (1974) :149–50.

[14]John Wilkinson, *Egeria's Travels* (London: SPCK, 1971), pp. 121–22. In a footnote, Wilkinson comments: "Marthana, like Macrina, sister of St. Basil of Caesarea and St. Gregory of Nyssa, was probably made a deaconess through the episcopal laying on of hands."

[15]Morris, *Against Nature and God,* p. 57.

[16]Bernadette Brooten, PhD. dissertation, Harvard Divinity School (Tübingen).

BIBLICAL EXEGESIS

THE KEY BIBLICAL passages which feature in the debate on women and church leadership are Genesis 1-3 and 1 Timothy 2:11-13; Ephesians 5:21-33 and 1 Peter 3:1-7; 1 Corinthians 11:3-16 and 1 Corinthians 14:33-36; and Galatians 3:28. These have been examined in numerous books and articles over the last decade, many of which are readily accessible to the general reader.[1] This chapter directs attention to some of the major issues and suggests guidelines toward the resolution of problems inherent in the text.

Genesis 1-3 and 1 Timothy 2:11-13

There is no more appropriate place to begin than the Genesis creation narratives. What storms of controversy have raged over such seemingly peaceful waters! "And there was evening and there was morning, a sixth day"—the crucial day of creation (Gen. 1:31). On that day "God created man in his own image, in the image of God he created him; male and female he created them" (Gen. 1:27). It is generally acknowledged that the Book of Genesis brings together two ancient creation narratives, one contained in Genesis 1:1–2:4a, the other contained in Genesis 2:4b-24. In the first narrative the creation of human life comes as the climax of the creative activity of God, after the creation of plants and animals. In the second narrative man is created first, then the trees and animals, and finally woman.

3

Stylistic variations also indicate that these treasures of early prose have come to us from two different sources. Chapter 3 contains the narrative of the sin of humankind and the exclusion of Adam and Eve from the presence of God. Here in poetic form a curse is pronounced over the serpent (Gen. 3:14-15), over the woman (Gen. 3:16), and over the man (Gen. 3:17-19).

What is the relationship between the creation narratives and the issue of women's leadership in the church? The debate consists of two major arguments. One argument concerns chronology. The second creation narrative states that man was created before woman and that woman was tempted and fell into sin before man. The writer of 1 Timothy 2 uses these facts in support of his statement that women should remain quiet in church. The other argument concerns the nature of the roles to be assumed by the male and the female. The creation narratives, say the scholars who uphold this viewpoint, portray a model which was intended by God to establish for all time the respective roles of man and woman. It is argued that this model should therefore be used as the basis for church structure. Both arguments are analyzed and discussed below.

In a passage dealing with the appropriate manner of conducting Christian worship, the writer of the Pastoral Epistles indicates that Christian women should be modestly dressed and should "learn in silence with all submissiveness." The writer adds, "I permit no woman to teach or to have authority over men." The reasoning adduced for this is, "For Adam was formed first, then Eve; and Adam was not deceived, but the woman was deceived and became a transgressor." Perhaps desiring to soften the impact of these words, the writer concludes, "Yet woman will be saved through bearing children, if she continues in faith and love and holiness, with modesty" (1 Tim. 2:11-15).[2]

The initial problem arises when the statement "Adam was formed first" is examined. Was the writer unaware of the creation narrative in Genesis 1? It is clear that the argument is dependent on a consideration of Genesis 2 alone. Even on this basis it is hard to imagine why the time difference in creation would become elevated into a principle that for all time accords to the woman a passive role in worship.

Perhaps this position can be supported by reference to the significant status of the firstborn in Jewish tradition. Particular honors, including the right of inheritance, accrued to the firstborn child. When Tamar gave birth to twins, the midwife was careful to tie a band around the arm of the "firstborn," although, as it happened, his twin brother was delivered first (Gen. 38:27-30). But, in the case of the twins born to Rebekah, it was the second child Jacob, not the firstborn Esau, who became the recipient of these special honors (Gen. 25:21-26). And Paul, commenting in Romans 9:10-13 on this strange turn of events in the history of his own nation, observes that the choice as to which of Rebekah's children was to be preeminent was made by God even before the twins were born. This choice had nothing whatever to do with their order of birth or their acts or attitudes. Paul sees this as an important principle in God's dealings with humankind. It is hard to imagine, then, why the priority in time reflected in the second creation narrative would carry the significance attributed to it in 1 Timothy 2:13.

The second line in this argument—"Adam was not deceived, but the woman was deceived"—is equally problematic. Genesis 3 clearly indicates that both the man and the woman participated in the forbidden act. Verse 6 reads: "She gave some also to her husband who was *with her*" (J.D.; the RSV is not precise at this point). The simple context of the passage assumes that the man was by her side while the preceding conversation was taking place. He therefore participated equally in her guilt. Indeed, if blame were to be apportioned one way or the other, it could be argued that the command "You shall not eat" (Gen. 2:17) was given, according to this second creation narrative, before the woman was even created. (In the first creation narrative there is no such command.) The woman had presumably heard it only from her husband. This would put the heavier load of responsibility on the man's shoulders—he had been given the command by God and was therefore sure of its origin. Interestingly enough, Paul, when commenting on this passage in Romans 5:12–21, lays the guilt for the act entirely on Adam and points out that it was through the transgression of that one *man* that death came to humankind.

If the writer's argument in 1 Timothy 2 seems obscure up to this point, his final comment occasions even more distress. Conditional on her holy manner of life, "woman will be saved through bearing children." As salvation through childbirth is not a recognized dogma of the Christian faith, Bible translators have used some ingenuity in communicating the meaning of this statement. Some assume the writer to mean that if the woman lives a holy life, she will be safely delivered when giving birth to a child. J. B. Phillips translates, "I believe that women will come safely through childbirth if they maintain a life of faith." The problem inherent in such a translation is obvious. The Christian woman who dies in childbirth has presumably not maintained a life of faith. Kenneth Taylor, the paraphraser of the Living Bible, is so acutely aware of the delicacy of the situation that he takes it on himself to insert a reading, not found to my knowledge in any ancient manuscript, which affirms the Pauline stance of salvation by faith alone. Taylor writes, "So God sent pain and suffering to women when their children are born, but he will save their souls if they trust in him, living quiet, good, and loving lives." It sounds good—at least it graciously assumes that women are included in God's great plan of salvation—but it simply is not what the biblical writer was saying. So the enigma remains.

What, then, can be learned from this particular exhortation in the Pastoral Epistles? Simply, that the writer felt it proper for Christian women to be modestly dressed and that he did not personally permit women to teach in the churches over which he exercised supervision. The passage indicates therefore that there were churches even in "liberated" Asia where women were not permitted to assume leadership roles. Read alongside passages such as 1 Corinthians 11:5, where it is clear that Paul did permit women to speak in his churches, it reminds us that in this matter, as in many others, there was a variety of practice in the apostolic church. Thus, caution should be exercised lest one particular ruling be treated as though it were the norm for all times and all places.

The second argument that arises from Genesis 1-3 is that the creation narratives supply the church with a model which establishes a kind of blueprint of the respective roles of men and women within the church. In the second creation narrative the writer describes how God desired to enrich the life of Adam. "Then the Lord God said, 'It is not good that the man should be alone; I will make him a helper fit for him'" (Gen. 2:18). In order to achieve this, God caused a deep sleep to fall on the man, and he removed a rib from his side. "The rib which the Lord God had taken from the man he made into a woman and brought her to the man" (Gen. 2:22).

It will be remembered that the first creation narrative describes the simultaneous creation of man and woman, but this second narrative is chosen by commentators to support certain views of male dominance and female subservience which have been very influential in Christian circles. Keil and Delitzsch, for example, commenting on this passage in 1864, write, "Of such a help the man stood in need, in order that he might fulfill *his* calling, not only to perpetuate and multiply *his* race, but to cultivate and govern the earth" (emphasis added). The same writers conclude from the "rib" method of creation, "By this the priority and superiority of the man, and the dependence of the woman upon the man, are established as an ordinance of divine creation."[3]

Are such viewpoints supported by the text in question? The expression used here to describe the woman, usually translated "a helper fit for [man]," is better translated "a helper corresponding to [man]." The idea communicated by the Hebrew is that woman is the counterpart of man in the same way that a wax seal becomes the counterpart of the design on a signet ring. She is not identical to man, but she is his exact counterpart. There is no suggestion of inferiority in this analogy. Nor does the use of the word *helper* designate the woman to a subordinate or dependent role. On the contrary, the word is used in the Hebrew Scriptures to describe a stronger party who comes in to support a weaker party, for example a nation which serves as an ally in time of war. In this connection God is spoken of as the "helper" of Israel. One of the sons of Zipporah and Moses was called Eliezer (Exod. 18:4), which means "My God (is) the helper." In the Song of Moses it is written:

> "There is none like God, O Jeshurun
> who rides through the heavens to your help,
> and in his majesty through the skies" (Deut. 33:26).

Thus the Genesis text under consideration actually represents man as the weaker partner. He stands in need of the strength which only woman can supply.

Other writers have directed attention to the fall narrative, claiming that it is an indication of the respective roles to be assumed by men and women. The curse pronounced over the woman reads:

> "In pain you shall bring forth children,
> yet your desire shall be for your husband,
> and he shall rule over you" (Gen. 3:16).

It is strange that the bringing forth of children would be considered a curse when children were regarded in that society as a rich blessing from God. The sexual desire of a woman for a man is also hard to understand as a curse. The thought seems to be that in spite of the pain associated with childbirth, a woman will still have sexual desire for a man and will participate with him in sexual union. In this sense he will have control over her. Paul has a similar turn of phrase in 1 Corinthians 7:4. Instructing that husbands and wives ought not to withhold their bodies from sexual union, Paul comments, "For the wife does not rule over her own body, but the husband does; likewise the husband does not rule over his own body, but the wife does." Paul identifies the woman's role as "ruling" over the man in this respect and does not find it incompatible with that of the man ruling over the woman. In like manner, one might assume that the writer of the Genesis passage did not intend it to be understood that men would not have sexual desire for their wives, or that a woman's sexual desire would necessarily be stronger than that of a man.

Commentators have not always directed attention to these aspects of the passage. Many have isolated "he shall rule over you" from its immediate context of intercourse, pregnancy, and birth and have conjured it into a specter of male dominance. In his *New Commentary on Genesis,* Delitzsch writes: "The woman will henceforth involuntarily follow the leading of the man, and be subject even against her will to his dominion. . . . The man may command as master, and the woman is bound externally and internally to obey."[4]

Calvin, commenting on this passage, concludes, "Thus the woman, who had perversely exceeded her proper bounds, is forced back to her own position. She had, indeed, previously been subject to her husband, but that was a liberal and gentle subjection; now, however, she is cast into servitude."[5] A rereading of Genesis 1:1–3:16 throws no light whatsoever on what Calvin describes as the "proper bounds" for woman. In Genesis 1:28 both the man and the woman are blessed by God and are jointly commanded to "be fruitful and multiply, and fill the earth and subdue it, and have dominion." Both are pronounced "very good" in the eyes of God (Gen. 1:31). In the second creation narrative the woman is described as a helper corresponding to the man, and the union of man and woman is described as becoming "one flesh" (Gen. 2:24). It is clear that the "liberal and gentle subjection" of which Calvin speaks is not featured in the text, and it is very doubtful indeed whether "cast into servitude" rightly paraphrases the author's intent in Genesis 3:16.

Interpretations such as Calvin's have proliferated in commentaries intended to enrich the sermon content of preachers. J. S. Exell, in his *Homiletical Commentary on Genesis,* writes: "Women are to be subject to their husbands. This is the law of God. This is the ordination of physical life and energy. And any man who allows his wife to habitually rule him reverses the law of God, and the curse of the fall."[6] Exell does emphasize, though, that "man is not to crush a woman into a slave"—a heartening comment. This verse may also be interpreted in the context of aetiology. The account has been described as a primitive attempt on the part of the Genesis narrator to explain certain phenomena which are hard to understand. "Why is it," people wonder, "that women have such pain when giving birth? Animals seem to give birth so much more easily." Or again, "Why is it that the woman's lot is frequently so degrading? Why is it that her work often amounts to slavery?" To such questions as these the Genesis narrator responds: "It is because of sin. God did not intend it to be that way."[7]

Thus we may conclude that if the phrase "he shall rule over you" refers to sexual powers, it is clear from Scripture and from experience that men and women are both subject to this kind of influence. In the woman's case, this can result in pregnancy and painful childbirth. If, however, the phrase "he shall rule over you" is a reference to the oppression women experience in a male-dominated culture, then the message of Genesis speaks clearly to the church of today—this is a manifestation of the activity of Satan and not of God. Those who argue that the church must preserve the status quo until the end time might consider whether this would also involve total dedication to natural childbirth and enforced manual labor in the fields. Such persons might also reflect on the extent to which the New Testament teaches that the "powers of the age to come" are operative in the world today. The church should surely be the first place in which these are seen to be effective.

It has become traditional to assume that the Genesis narrative of the fall portrays man as the dominant figure with woman usurping his authority. Such an assumption does not do justice to the evidence. If the text is allowed to speak for itself it will be seen that it was the woman who was approached when a decision was to be made that affected the husband and wife jointly (the verbs in Gen. 3:5 are second person plural); and it was the woman who ate first and afterwards gave food to the man. The woman is cast in the role of the curious, aggressive personality, the man assumes a passive stance—he eats without question.

Although this interpretation has become obscured through the passage of time, it features in at least one early writing, the *Anagogicarum Contemplationum* of Anastasius Sinaita. This document dates from the time of Irenaeus and has recently been the subject of an excellent critical note by Jean M. Higgins in the *Journal of Biblical Literature*.[8] (This note deals with the concept of "helper" as used in the *LXX* and early literature, a topic discussed above.) Higgins translates from Anastasius Sinaita as follows:

> For she [Eve] alone stood up to the serpent. She ate from the tree, but with resistance and dissent, and after being dealt with perfidiously. But Adam partook of the fruit given by the woman, without even beginning to make a fight, without a word of contradiction—a perfect demonstration of consummate weakness and a cowardly soul.

This dominant role assumed by the woman accords well with the marriage pattern outlined in Genesis 2:24, "Therefore a man leaves his father and his mother and cleaves to his wife and the two become one flesh." In a patriarchal society such as that of the Hebrews it is amazing to find preserved in these early traditions a reference to the fact that it was the man who left home and family to live with his wife, rather than vice versa. The statement that they became "one flesh," suggesting total absorption in one another and therefore equality, is also illuminating. The man does not possess the woman but becomes a part of her. This material, however, deals with the male/female relationship within the context of marriage and does not necessarily have anything to say concerning the participation of either within the context of church leadership, even though it has often been used to that effect.

Ephesians 5:21–33 and 1 Peter 3:1–7

The husband/wife relationship is the subject of discussion in Ephesians 5:21–33 and 1 Peter 3:1–7, but these two passages are often referred to as guidelines for male/female roles within the church. In Ephesians 5:21–25 believers are exhorted:

> Be subject to one another out of reverence for Christ. Wives, be subject to your husbands, as to the Lord. For the husband is the head of the wife as Christ is the head of the church, his body, and is himself its Savior. As the church is subject to Christ, so let wives also be subject in everything to their husbands. Husbands, love your wives, as Christ loved the church and gave himself up for her.

In 1 Peter 3:1, 6–7 these instructions are given:

> Likewise you wives, be submissive to your husbands. . . . Sarah obeyed Abraham, calling him lord. And you are now her children. . . . Likewise you husbands, live considerately with your wives, bestowing honor on the woman as the weaker sex, since you are joint heirs of the grace of life.

Two issues arise from these passages: first, the nature of the relationship between husband and wife suggested here, and second, the connection, if any, between these guidelines and those to be adopted in assigning leadership roles in the church.

In the Ephesians passage the writer's introductory command is that mutual subjection is to be the rule in Christian marriage.[9] This concept of mutual subjection is addressed specifically to wives (Eph. 5:22–24) and to husbands (Eph. 5:25–30).

The instruction to wives is brief and amounts only to a statement to the effect that they should acknowledge the "headship" of their husbands. What this implies is not elaborated on except by analogy—as the church is subject to Christ, so a wife must be subject to her husband. In what way is the church subject to Christ? A difficult question to answer because the church is in fact "his body" (Eph. 5:23) and therefore so closely identified with him that distinctions become confusing. The letter which embodies this passage is so overwhelmingly enthusiastic and positive about the concept of the church, so full of joyful affirmation, that little is said which depicts what we understand by "subjection." The church participates with Christ in spiritual blessings (1:3), experiences his power as a life-giving force (1:19–2:10), is joined with Christ in a structure of which he is the cornerstone (2:19-22), and is saturated so deeply in the love of Christ that God himself becomes accessible to her (3:17-19). It is Christ who supplies the energy for her spiritual growth (4:15-16), and the church must learn to live in a way that is pleasing to him (5:10).

The instruction to husbands is more explicit. The analogy is that the husband is to exercise "headship" in the same way that Christ exercises headship over the church. The writer elaborates on this clearly. Christ's love for the church was so self-negating that it led him to lay down his life on her behalf. In the same way, the love of the husband for the wife is to be such that if it comes to a choice, the husband will be prepared to lay down his life on her behalf. The wife's well-being is to be his consuming passion. Thus the husband's headship finds its practical application in an attitude of subjection. The writer of Ephesians draws the passage to a close with a reiteration of Genesis 2:24, "the two shall become one flesh," exhorting that this must be actualized by the practice of mutual submission outlined above.

Thus the Ephesians passage teaches mutual submission between husband and wife. This will be, as in the case of Christ and the church, the natural concomitant of mutual love. The sexual union of husband and wife is in some mysterious sense an image of the close relationship between Christ and the church, a relationship so intimate and so profoundly potent that it becomes a living organism, growing and developing with the life-giving powers of God himself. Headship and subjection are to be understood in this context.

The comments in 1 Peter concern an entirely different situation. Here it is implied that the wives addressed are those whose husbands are not Christians. These men have heard the preaching of the gospel but have remained nonbelievers. Perhaps the manner of life exemplified in their wives will persuade them of the reality of Christian experience. The reference to Sarah is perplexing, but the comment that she called Abraham "lord" indicates that the writer had in mind Genesis 18:12. The Hebrew word *Adoni* is used widely in the Hebrew Scriptures. It may refer to Yahweh himself, it may be used as a general title of respect (as in Gen. 18:3 where Abraham uses the same word to address his three mysterious visitors), or it may (as here) serve as a synonym for husband. Indeed, the RSV translates the phrase "my husband is old" rather than "my lord being old" (as in the KJV), so commonly is it found with this meaning. The fact that Sarah used such a word with reference to her husband in no way suggests that the relationship between them was that of slave to master.

Nor does the Genesis passage give any indication that Sarah "obeyed" Abraham. Perhaps the writer of 1 Peter had in mind the fact that although Sarah considered herself past childbearing age, she yet "submitted" herself sexually to her husband and as a result conceived a child. In any case, the character sketch of Sarah in these early narratives is far from what is today envisaged in the term "submissive wife." In Genesis 21 Sarah is depicted in the role of decision maker. Although her strategy was very displeasing to Abraham, Abraham felt constrained to obey her. "God said to Abraham, . . . 'Whatever Sarah says to you, do as she tells you'" (Gen. 21:12). Sarah's decision in this instance affected the destiny of the entire Hebrew nation.

The final comment in the 1 Peter passage—"husbands, live considerately with your wives, bestowing honor on the woman as the weaker sex, since you are joint heirs of the grace of life"—also requires examination. In what sense is the woman to be considered "weaker" than the man? Physically? Intellectually? Morally? In all probability it is physical weakness that the writer has in mind; it was customary in those times to regard women as unable to carry on normal lives during menstruation and pregnancy. But because these physical limitations were directed to such a noble end, women were to be regarded with honor.

This thought accords very well with the sentiment expressed by Paul in 1 Corinthians 12:22-23, 25:

> The parts of the body which seem to be weaker are indispensable, and those parts of the body which we think less honorable we invest with the greater honor . . . that there may be no discord in the body, but that the members may have the same care for one another.

The 1 Peter narrative concludes with a similar call to unity: Husband and wife are "joint heirs of the grace of life," and the entire church community is exhorted to demonstrate "unity of spirit, sympathy, love of the brethren, a tender heart and a humble mind" (1 Peter 3:8). In the human body the apparent weakness of an organ does not mean that it is in any way inferior. Indeed, it may be more essential than a stronger organ, as the heart is more essential than the rib cage that protects it. So the fact that the woman from time to time endures periods of physical weakness does not in any way lessen the honor due her; rather, it enhances this.

These passages under consideration have to do with the relationship of husband and wife. Do they embody any principles which apply to the respective roles of men and women in the context of the church? The analogy of the church as the bride of Christ, implied in Ephesians 5:31-32, does not help a great deal, for it describes the relationship of the men and women who comprise the church with Christ, the one who "nourishes and cherishes" it. There seems to be no indication in either Ephesians or 1 Peter that these comments regarding husband/wife relationships should be used as a basis for role distinction in a church context. Indeed, when these passages are analyzed, the overwhelming impression seems to be one of role identity rather than role distinction. Even so, the texts speak in the context of family life and do not give any hint that they embody principles which are to be applied specifically to church leadership functions. Naturally, mutual submission and mutual love would be commendable under any circumstances and are not to be excluded from the church context, but that is to speak in a more general manner.

1 Corinthians 11:3-16 and 1 Corinthians 14:33-36

These passages in Paul's letter to the Corinthian church have given rise to all manner of controversy over the role of women in the church. Because the lines of argument in 1 Corinthians 11:3-16 are somewhat complicated, and because the ideas expressed in 1 Corinthians 14:33-36 have sometimes been taken out of context, Christians have arrived at quite differing interpretations of "what Paul actually meant." To this day these passages are used by some to support the notion that women should cover their heads with a hat or scarf when entering a church building, and by others to "prove conclusively" that women are forever denied ordination as ministers.[10]

There is no doubt that the 1 Corinthians 11 passage has to do with public gatherings of the church for the purpose of worship. Paul's instructions cover not only the appropriate manner of dress on such occasions but also the proper administration of the eucharist and the effective use of spiritual gifts within the community. In the passage under consideration, 1 Corinthians 11:3-16, the focus is on the way men and women should be attired when leading the congregation in prayer and prophecy. The comment, "any woman who prays or prophesies with her head unveiled dishonors her head" (1 Cor. 11:5), indicates that women were taking part in the leadership of church worship in Corinth. If Paul had disapproved of this, it would have been natural for him to express such disapproval here. He did not hesitate to voice disapproval over other issues (cf. 1 Cor. 11:21-22). The fact that he takes care to explain the customary manner of dress for women leading in such capacities indicates that the practice was a normal one in the Pauline churches.

Both the nature of the activity and the manner of dress recommended indicate that women were participating orally in gatherings of the church in which both men and women were present. With respect to "prophesying," the writer of Acts (2:14–21) recalls that Peter, in his Pentecostal sermon, saw in the infant church's experience of the Holy Spirit a fulfillment of the words of the prophet Joel: "Your sons and your daughters shall prophesy" (Joel 2:28). What was the nature of this activity? According to 1 Corinthians 14:3, the one "who prophesies speaks to men for their upbuilding and encouragement and consolation." Prophesying edifies the church (1 Cor. 14:4). It also convicts the unbeliever: "The secrets of his heart are disclosed; and so, falling on his face, he will worship God and declare that God is really among you" (1 Cor. 14:25). Prophecy thus embodies the elements of Christian teaching and Christian preaching. It is teaching or preaching communicated orally to a congregation in a language understood by those present. Paul instructs, "You can all prophesy one by one, so that all may learn and all be encouraged" (1 Cor. 14:31).

In giving instructions about appropriate dress, Paul states that whereas a man should have his head uncovered when participating in worship, a woman should wear a veil. This might have been a reflection of local custom. Certainly in first-century Judaism a married woman was required to cover her hair and chin when appearing in public; not to do so was considered a serious affront to her husband's honor. In spite of her newfound freedom in Christ, the Christian woman must not transgress recognized standards of decorum in her own society. This would seem reasonable, and the principle could be adapted to any such societal custom. However, this does not mean that Christian women should perpetuate customs that reflect standards of decorum of a bygone age rather than those of the society in which they find themselves. If, for example, women in a Western church decided to follow the apostle's advice literally and began to wear veils for public worship, they would create the very situation the apostle was seeking to avoid. "Outsiders" would begin to question the strange customs accompanying the Christian faith and might thereby be discouraged from becoming members of the Christian community.[11]

Generally speaking, the stumbling block in this passage is not the principle, but the reasons Paul adduces in support of the principle: "The head of every man is Christ, the head of a woman is her husband, and the head of Christ is God" (1 Cor. 11:3), and "a man ought not to cover his head, since he is the image and glory of God; but a woman is the glory of man" (1 Cor. 11:7).

The first phrase demanding examination is the apparent hierarchy, God—Christ—Man—Woman. The word *head* here must be understood not as "ruler" but as "source." Christ came from God; he is "the only Son from the Father" (John 1:14). As the agent of creation (John 1:3) Christ brought man into being ("humankind," of course, according to Genesis 1, but Paul emphasizes the male of the species here); and from the male of the species, the female came into being (Gen. 2:21-22). Paul's uneasiness with drawing implications from this pattern has been observed earlier. He hastens to add that whatever the second creation narrative might indicate, "in the Lord woman is not independent of man nor man of woman; for as woman was made from man, so man is now born of woman" (1 Cor. 11:11).

Similar problems arise in the second phrase, that man is "the image and glory of God; but woman is the glory of man." In Genesis 1:27 it is clear that the image of God is borne by both the male and the female of the species. Paul is sensitive to this and does not push his argument to imply that the woman bears the image of the man (a statement which, of course, would be incorrect). The contrast presented to the reader is the concept of "glory," about which the creation narratives say nothing but rabbinic tradition says much.

Because woman is the glory of man, Paul writes, a woman must cover her head when leading public worship. Why? M. D.

Hooker finds the key to this issue in verse 10: "That is why a woman ought to have authority (not 'a veil' as RSV) on her head, because of the angels." Leaving aside the matter of the identity of "the angels," in what way is the veil a symbol of "authority"? Hooker observes that in Middle Eastern culture the veil was a symbol of subservience. The argument seems to be that the man's head must remain uncovered because he is a reflection of God's glory; the woman, however, is the glory of man. Such glory must be covered when a woman leads a worshiping congregation, because in this role she stands not in relation to her husband but in relation to God. The veil has become for her a symbol of her new-found authority. "If now woman also, in contrast to Jewish custom, takes part in prayer and prophecy, this is because a new power has been given to her."[12]

Thus, this passage, 1 Corinthians 11:3–16, speaks clearly to the issue of women exercising leadership functions in the church. Although there are differences in creation, which must be preserved in modes of dress, men and women stand before God as equals. Women, however, should be careful not to use this new-found authority to transgress the boundaries of social convention in a manner that would cause offense to those who are outside the Christian community.

Is it possible to reconcile this perspective with Paul's exhortation in 1 Corinthians 14:34–36: "The women should keep silence in the churches. For they are not permitted to speak, but should be subordinate. . . . It is shameful for a woman to speak in church"?

John Calvin, writing in 1546, sees no dichotomy between these two passages. Both, in his opinion, clearly teach that women are inferior to men and should not participate in Christian worship. Calvin defines prayer and prophecy in terms of public leadership and teaching: And it is his opinion that Paul only reproves the women for prophesying with uncovered heads; he does not give them permission to prophesy in some other way! "The woman," Calvin writes, "derives her origin from the man; she is therefore inferior in rank." He continues, "On this account all women are born, that they may acknowledge themselves inferior in consequence of the superiority of the male sex."[13] Women, however, must not allow that thought to distress them: "Let the woman be satisfied with her state of subjection, and not take it amiss that she is made inferior to the more distinguished sex." This "more distinguished sex" alone is responsible for a church's teaching ministry, because "the office of teaching is a superiority in the Church," and "if the woman is under subjection, she is, consequently, prohibited from authority to teach in public."[14]

As if to support his own argument from an appeal to "custom," Calvin states: "Unquestionably, wherever even natural propriety has been maintained, women have in all ages been excluded from the public management of affairs. It is the dictate of common sense that female government is improper and unseemly."[15] Such a comment gives insight into the true source of Calvin's convictions. Rather than stemming from the biblical tradition, they reflect the opinions of a society in which for many years women had been subjugated and oppressed. Society molded Calvin's concept of a woman's role, and he read this concept into the biblical text. How could Calvin have conceived the possibility of an Indira Gandhi or a Golda Meir or a Margaret Thatcher? Fortunately, present-day commentators are less bound to cultural norms and more free to permit the biblical text to speak for itself.

As the natural reading of 1 Corinthians 11:3–16 is that women did pray and prophesy in the Pauline churches, it is generally accorded that the instruction in 1 Corinthians 14:33–36 cannot refer to such leadership functions. Paul was not likely to contradict himself so completely. This particular instruction comes in the context of practices, involving both men and women, which were disruptive of the orderly conduct of church worship. Some were speaking in tongues with no indication of the meaning of the words being spoken. This, Paul states, is not helpful when Christians have gathered to learn from one another. Some, considering themselves to be "inspired by God" and unable to hold back their "spiritual" utterances, were interrupting other speakers to superimpose their own "messages." Paul exhorts them to exercise restraint. The situation involving the women, then, may well have resulted from some purely local problem that was disruptive of the worship situation. Perhaps women were chattering among themselves? More likely, a group of women were asking questions in a disorderly manner, perhaps challenging comments made by their husbands. This gave a bad impression of Christian relationships. Society demanded that a woman be supportive of her husband. If there were issues of debate, they would be dealt with best in the privacy of the home.

The Corinthian texts dealt with here must be weighed against one another. Paul affirmed the leadership role assumed by women in public worship in the church of Corinth. His concern was only that proper decorum should accompany leadership activity. The exhortation that women should remain silent has reference to a particular situation in which certain women were creating disorder in a congregational setting. This, Paul maintained, should not be permitted under any circumstances.

Galatians 3:28

Probably the most profound New Testament insight regarding the respective status of men and women in the Christian community is found in Galatians 3:28:

> There is neither Jew nor Greek, there is neither slave nor free, there is neither male nor female; for you are all one in Christ Jesus.

In the society of Paul's day there was a tremendous difference in the sense of personal worth and human dignity between the paired categories of people mentioned here. It was taken for granted that the Jew was superior to the Greek, the freeman to the slave, the male to the female. The message of Christ, however, was the great equalizer. In Christ, each person stood before God as an individual of worth independent of race, status, or sex. It was to be the mission of the Christian faith to live out this concept, even within the complexities of its contemporary situation. In fact, it was precisely in those complexities that the Christian church was to demonstrate to the world the truth of this astounding reality. And the church of today is still presented with this same challenge.

Notes

[1]See the excellent bibliography compiled by Donald Dayton in *Chauvinist or Feminist? Paul's View of Women,* by Richard and Joyce Boldry (Grand Rapids: Baker, 1976), pp. 73–82. See also Dennis Kuhns, *Women in the Church* (Scottdale, Pa.: Herald Press, 1978); Don Williams, *The Apostle Paul and Women in the Church* (Van Nuys, Calif.: BIM, 1977); and Paul K. Jewett, *The Ordination of Women* (Grand Rapids: Eerdmans, 1980).

[2]For a most perceptive commentary on this passage, see Aida Besancon Spencer, "Eve at Ephesus," *Journal of the Evangelical Theological Society* 17, no. 4 (Fall 1974): 215–22.

[3]C. F. Keil and F. Delitzsch, *Biblical Commentary on the Old Testament, The Pentateuch,* trans. James Martin (Edinburg: T. & T. Clark, 1864), 1:86–89.

[4]Franz Delitzsch, *A New Commentary on Genesis,* trans. Sophia Taylor (Edinburg: T. & T. Clark, 1888), 1:166.

[5]John Calvin, *Commentaries on the First Book of Moses Called Genesis,* trans. John King (Grand Rapids: Eerdmans, 1948), 1:172.

[6]J. S. Exell, *Homiletical Commentary on Genesis* (New York: Funk & Wagnalls, 1892), pp. 66–67.

[7]For a more detailed discussion of this interpretation see Gerhard von Rad, *Genesis, A Commentary,* trans. John H. Marks (Philadelphia: Westminster, 1961), pp. 90–93.

[8]*Journal of Biblical Literature* 97/2 (1978): 253–56.

[9]The NIV obscures this thought by treating 5:21 as though it were a part of the preceding paragraph. The reasoning behind such a decision is that in the Greek the verb "be subject" here is a participle rather than an imperative and would therefore need to be dependent on a main verb. However, in the context of exhortation, as here, the participle may be used as an independent verb, in which case it serves as an imperative. (Cf. C. Leslie Mitton, *New Century Bible, Ephesians* [London: Oliphants, 1976], p. 195). It seems to me that the sense of the passage demands that verse 21 be linked closely with the verses following. For reflection on this concept of mutual submission in marriage, see Patricia Gundry, *Heirs Together* (Grand Rapids: Zondervan, 1980).

[10]Much research has been carried out in relation to 1 Corinthians, and excellent commentaries and articles are readily available. Particularly valuable are these commentaries: F. F. Bruce, *New Century Bible, 1 and 2 Corinthians* (London: Oliphants, 1971), see pp. 102–8, 135–36; C. K. Barrett, *A Commentary on the First Epistle to the*

Corinthians (New York: Harper & Row, 1968), see pp. 246-58, 330-34; W. F. Orr and J. A. Walther, *The Anchor Bible, I Corinthians* (New York: Doubleday, 1976), see pp. 258-64, 311-15. In addition, the reader might consult an article written by M. D. Hooker, "Authority on Her Head: An Examination of I Cor. xi.10," *New Testament Studies* 10 (1963-64): 410-16. In this brief consideration it would be impossible to do justice to the wealth of material available; it must suffice to cover some of the more obvious problems, giving a perspective from which they may be explored.

[11]Until recently a similar situation was reflected in some churches over the issue of women wearing slacks when attending church. This was considered to be "men's clothing" and was forbidden on the basis of Deuteronomy 22:5, "A woman shall not wear anything that pertains to a man, nor shall a man put on a woman's garment." Such churches overlooked (a) the fact that the writer of the Deuteronomy passage had something quite different in mind, and (b) the fact that both men's and women's fashions change with the passage of time. There is no religious virtue whatsoever in being "behind the fashion."

[12]Hooker, "Authority on Her Head," p. 415.

[13]John Calvin, *Commentary on the Corinthians,* trans. John Pringle (Grand Rapids: Eerdmans, 1948), 1:355-58.

[14]Calvin, *Corinthians,* 1:361, 468.

[15]Calvin, *Corinthians,* 1:468.

THE CHURCH LEADER: TITLE AND FUNCTION

RELIGIOUS GROUPS ORGANIZED for worship and service find it necessary to develop leadership structures. Leaders are given titles, and the functions associated with these titles are outlined. Leadership positions are regarded with respect, and generally allowance is made for the differing abilities of the people who assume leadership roles. Today the various denominations of the church have well-established patterns of leadership. These have evolved over a period of time and are often colored as much by unwritten assumptions as by written precepts. Often one such unwritten assumption is that the church leaders should be male.

Guidelines

When considering the role of women in church leadership, it is important to assess realistically the leadership situations found in the churches of New Testament times. Does the New Testament present guidelines concerning leadership structure? Is there in the New Testament a "blueprint" which should be used at all times and in all places when structuring Christian community? It would seem natural to turn to the pages of the New Testament for guidelines concerning such. The reader will find, however, that guidelines are hard to establish, except in the most general way. Although written well after the establishment of the early Chris- tian communities, the Gospels give little indication how those communities were led. Jesus evidently chose the Twelve to be his inner circle of disciples (Mark 3:13-19), and on occasion they were the particular recipients of his teachings (Mark 8:27-33). Among these, three people—Peter, James, and John—were singled out at various times (Mark 9:2-13; 14:33). Occasionally Peter alone received special commendation (Matt. 16:16-19). Luke's Gospel refers to a wider group—the Seventy—who were divided into teams of two and were sent out to proclaim the message of Jesus and to heal (Luke 10:1-16).

The Book of Acts presents a slightly more structured situation, mentioning "apostles and elders" and "prophets and teachers" in connection with local communities (Acts 15:2; 13:1). After his missionary tour in Asia, Paul is said to have returned to the several towns in which groups of people had embraced the Christian faith in order to appoint "elders" who were presumably to assume responsibility for nurturing these small congregations (14:21-23).

But the New Testament letters are curiously silent about the leadership structure of the church. For example, in 1 Corinthians, a very personal letter from Paul to a church which he himself had established and with which he was well acquainted, there is no reference at all to any official leader. This is all the more surprising in view of the special nature of the problems in the Corinthian church. Many of these stemmed from a lack of organization and supervision, the very areas in which one would expect leaders to be assuming responsibility. Even when Paul advises that a special church meeting be called to deal with a serious matter of discipline, he addresses his comments to the whole church and makes no mention of a specific person whose responsibility it might have been to take action (1 Cor. 5:1-8).

The letter to the Hebrews does mention church leaders, although only briefly. "Obey your leaders and submit to them; for they are keeping watch over your souls, as men who will have to give account" (Heb. 13:17). First Peter includes a special exhortation to "the elders among you." They are to "tend the flock of God that is [their] charge, not by constraint but willingly, not for shameful gain but eagerly, not as domineering over those in [their] charge but being examples to the flock" (1 Peter 5:2). Comments such as these give some insight into the nature of a church leader's responsibility, but they are not at all specific concerning either office or function.

The Pastoral epistles, the only canonical letters addressed to a church leader, reflect a more structured situation. Timothy has been left in Ephesus to supervise the churches there, and Titus has been given a similar task with respect to the churches on the island of Crete (1 Tim. 1:3; Titus 1:5). Instructions are given to these men concerning the appointment of church leaders, and the titles "bishop," "deacon," and "elder" emerge as referring to some particular church office. But the instructions given are more concerned with the qualities required of a person appointed to such office than with specific function, so that once again the reader is left to surmise the content of the office.

At the outset, then, it is important to note that there is no clear pattern for church leadership laid down in the New Testament documents with respect to either title or function. Various people are described as "apostle," "prophet," "teacher," "bishop," "deacon," or "elder," but the exact nature of their duties is nowhere spelled out. At most, these titles can be examined to establish their significance, and the passages referring to each can be explored for some indication of function. But the strong possibility remains that there was no standard practice of leadership in the early church and that initially title and function varied from place to place. The needs of the individual community determined the nature of the leadership function. Awareness of this fact is important. It suggests that the church of today should also feel free to exercise that same creative influence. The office of church leadership is not static, prescribed by sacred decree, and unchangeable. It is a service-centered office which must always remain flexible enough to adapt to changing needs and changing opportunities.

Apostle, Prophet, Teacher

Writing to the Corinthian church, Paul states, "God has appointed in the church first apostles, second prophets, third teachers" (1 Cor. 12:28). The context of this statement deals with charismatic activity, and the statement itself is not necessarily a pronouncement about ecclesiastical structure. But could it be that in the early years of the church, when itinerant messengers of the gospel were essential, this was the nature of church leadership, while at a later, more settled stage, resident leaders such as bishops and deacons came into being?

The prophets of the New Testament communities, like the prophets of Old Testament times, evidently fulfilled a twofold ministry: the proclamation of God's message both in word and in action. According to 1 Corinthians 14 the gift of prophecy was widespread and was indeed a gift to be coveted. The outcome of the exercise of this charisma was that Christians were built up in their faith and non-Christians were confronted with the immediacy of God's presence (1 Cor. 14:3, 24-25).

The Book of Acts and other early Christian writings seem to indicate that some individuals were endowed with this charisma in a special way and received recognition as prophets and prophetesses. Their ministry included perceptive foresight and direction concerning the future. The prophet Agabus, one of a group of prophets in Jerusalem, informed the church of Antioch that there would be a time of famine. As a result, this church took steps to aid the Christians in Jerusalem (Acts 11:27-30). Agabus came down to Caesarea from Jerusalem with a prophetic message for Paul. Binding his own hands and feet with Paul's girdle, he warned the Christians of Paul's impending imprisonment (Acts 21:10-11). In Caesarea, Paul stayed in the home of Philip, whose four daughters were known as prophetesses (Acts 21:8-9). The church of Antioch was led by a group of "prophets and teachers" (Acts 13:1).

There is some overlap in function between the ministry of a prophet and that of an apostle. The apostles, for example, were involved in a ministry of evangelism (Acts 3:19-26) just as the prophets were (1 Cor. 14:24-25). They were also involved in a ministry of teaching (Acts 2:42) as were the prophets (1 Cor. 14:4). But the apostolic office emerged from the first-century church with clearer definition than the prophetic office, and it has assumed a greater significance.

Who were the apostles? And what was the exact nature of their ministry? The Lukan writings, particularly Acts, show much interest in this office. Jesus, after a night of prayer, selected from his circle of followers a group of twelve whom he named "apostles" (Luke 6:12-16). These twelve accompanied Jesus on his travels and were the special recipients of his teaching. They were commissioned to preach the kingdom of God and to carry out a ministry of healing (Luke 9:1-6). The apostles were also the recipients of post-resurrection teaching from Jesus (Acts 1:3), and they were at that time commissioned to a ministry of witness that was to embrace the whole world (Acts 1:8).

There are, however, some problems underlying this material. The number twelve was evidently very significant to the early church, so much so that the death of Judas occasioned the appointment of another disciple to take his place (Acts 1:15-26). Of the people who had accompanied the apostles from the time of Jesus' baptism, Matthias was chosen to "become with us a witness to his resurrection." But the Twelve as such seem to have faded very early from the memory of the early church. Even the listing of their names shows some confusion (Matt. 10:2-4; Mark 3:16-19; Luke 6:14–16). And although their commission was to evangelize the world, most of the Twelve apparently remained in Jerusalem. Peter and John went to Samaria only after a church had already been planted there (Acts 8:14-17); and if the tradition of Peter's later death in Rome is well-founded, it indicates only that he came to the heart of the Roman Empire long after the Christian church had been established in Italy. There is no reliable tradition that Peter ever held a leadership position in the church of Rome. John apparently traveled to Ephesus and assumed responsibility for the church in Asia Minor. The legendary material which asserts that other members of the Twelve founded churches throughout the world may be dismissed.[1]

The writings of Paul reflect a wider understanding of apostleship. No longer is it limited to the Twelve. Paul speaks of himself as an apostle, and he claims that his vision of the risen Christ, his mission to the Gentiles, and his constant sufferings, validate his apostleship. Paul names Barnabas, Andronicus, and Junia as apostles (1 Cor. 9:5-6; Rom. 16:7) and constantly assumes the existence of a wider group of apostles than that of the Twelve, both in Jerusalem (1 Cor. 15:5, 7) and elsewhere (2 Cor. 8:23). It was Paul, indeed, who carried forward most effectively the apostolic mission to be a witness "to the end of the earth" (Acts 1:8), and in doing this he was accompanied by people who had not been the recipients of the original commission nor necessarily in touch with those who had been the original recipients.[2] Writings such as the *Didache* show that in this wider sense the office of apostle continued at least into the second century C.E. (*Did.* 11:3-6).

The New Testament documents, then, reflect some diversity in the understanding of the apostolic function. Tension existed from time to time between those who were "reputed to be pillars" in the early church and those who were also apostles (Gal. 2). To overlook this in the early stages of the church's development is to do a disservice to the church of today. Office and function were not clearly defined, even in relation to such a significant office as that of apostle.

Was the apostolic office later passed on to other leaders in the church? In a concise volume, *Priest and Bishop, Biblical Reflections,* Raymond Brown, a Roman Catholic scholar, addresses himself to the question, "Are the bishops the successors of the apostles?"[3] Brown draws attention to the fact that little if anything is said in the

New Testament concerning the sacramental powers of apostles. Although it is known that they baptized, it is not conclusive that they presided at the eucharist or that they forgave sins. Nor is there any evidence that such sacramental powers were passed on to the Christian community in direct lineal contact with the apostles. Although it is intrinsically probable that some bishops may have been appointed by missionary apostles, this cannot be clearly demonstrated.

Added to this, Brown demonstrates that the task of the apostle differed from that of the bishop. While the apostle was of necessity a theological innovator, the bishop tended to become a preserver of the established tradition. So also the gifts needed for an itinerant ministry of evangelism differed from those needed for the pastoral supervision of a local congregation. Indeed, Brown claims, "In the modern church some of the principal activities of the Pauline apostolate, especially as regards leadership to face new religious problems, have been taken over functionally by men and women who are not bishops—by theologians, by enterprising priests . . . and by perceptive laity with their manifold competencies."[4]

Hans Küng asserts that apostleship per se can never be repeated.[5] What does remain is a task and a commission. The church as a whole is called to fulfill the task originally assigned to the apostles. Each member of the church must witness to a faith that is true to Scripture and must serve in submission to Christ. Küng concludes, "As an individual Christian, I must become a true successor of the Apostles; I must hear their witness, believe their message, imitate their mission and ministry."[6]

Bishop/Presbyter

Although two distinct titles—"bishop" *(episcopos)* and "presbyter" *(presbyteros,* elder)—occur in the New Testament documents, it is not at all clear that these represent different offices in the early church. When Paul made one last visit to the west coast of Asia, he called together the "presbyters" of the Ephesian church

(Acts 20:17) and reminded them that the Holy Spirit had placed them over the congregation as "bishops" (Acts 20:28). The "presbyters" addressed in 1 Peter 5:1 are exhorted to act as "bishops" in exercising oversight (1 Peter 5:2). And in the Pastoral Epistles, Titus is first instructed that his duty is to appoint "presbyters" and is then given guidelines concerning the qualities one should take into consideration when appointing a "bishop" (Titus 1:5–9). Were these terms always interchangeable, or did two originally distinct offices become merged into one?

It has been suggested that the concept of "presbyter" emerged from the Jewish Christian community in Jerusalem and that the designation "bishop" reflects the terminology of a Greek environment and of the Gentile world. This commonly held view has been challenged recently by Raymond Brown. Brown asserts that it is by chance that only the presbyters at Ephesus are referred to as bishops. It is equally likely that the Jerusalem presbyters were so designated but that this escaped mention in Acts. In addition, Brown finds in the Qumran community, a Jewish sectarian group, an office which closely parallels that of bishop. The *paqid* who presided over the Qumran community assembly functioned as a steward and manager and was responsible for instructing the community in the Law. These are the functions of a Christian bishop (Titus 1:7; 1 Tim. 3:4–5; Titus 1:9–10). Moreover, like the Christian bishop, the Qumran leader is symbolically described as "shepherd" (CD 13:9–10; cf. Acts 20:28; 1 Peter 5:2–4). Thus both the offices of presbyter and bishop may have originated from within the ranks of the Jewish Christians.[7]

The word *bishop (episcopos)* was borrowed by the Christians from the secular realm. In nonbiblical Greek it describes an onlooker or protector. When used of an officeholder, it has reference to a quite ordinary position usually involving technical or financial responsibilities. In the fifth century B.C.E. the title was used of officials sent from Athens to supervise members of the Attic league and to ensure public order. These "bishops" were somewhat resented by the towns that received them. The verb *episcopeo* is used by Aristophanes of the goddess Pallas Athena who watched over and therefore protected the Athenian fleet. In classical Greek this same verb is used with reference to visiting those who are sick in order to care for them or, in the case of a doctor, to aid in their healing. Thus the word *bishop* already had the connotations of management, supervision, and protection long before it was used as a title of a leader in a Christian community.

In the Septuagint, the Greek translation of the Hebrew Scriptures, *episcopos* is used in a similar way. Generally it means "overseer" or "supervisor." Eleazar as bishop was to assume responsibility for the tabernacle—the holy vessels, the oil, the incense, and the cereal offering (Num. 3:32; 4:16). At the time of Josiah's reformation, bishops were appointed to supervise the payment of money to the craftsmen working on the temple repairs (2 Chron. 34:12, 17). God, of course, is the absolute supervisor of men, and in Jewish thought he is described as *panepiscopos*. The land given to the Hebrews was his particular sphere of responsibility, and he looked down on it graciously, making it fruitful (Deut. 11:12).

In the New Testament the noun *episcopos* occurs only six times. In 1 Peter 2:25 it is used with reference to God and is linked with the concept of shepherd: "You were straying like sheep, but have now returned to the Shepherd and Guardian [bishop] of your souls." The same symbolism is found in Acts 20:28: "Take heed to yourselves and to all the flock, in which the Holy Spirit has made you overseers [bishops] to care for [shepherd] the church." In Philippians 1:1 the bishops (and deacons) of the church are named among the addressees of the letter. This is unique in the Pauline correspondence. It is notable that this one congregation had several bishops as well as several deacons.

The Pastoral Epistles are more specific in their use of the term. In 1 Timothy 3:1-7 (cf. Titus 1:5-9), Paul describes the qualities required of a person appointed to this office. It is assumed that the bishop will be married. His family life will be the testing ground for his aptitude in caring for the church. Self-control must be evident in all areas of his life, his relationship with other Christians must be exemplary, and he must have good rapport with people both informally (in hospitality) and formally (in teaching). He must be mature in Christian experience, and he must be well-respected in the community outside the church. Little is said concerning the nature or duties of the office.

The presbyter (or elder) is mentioned more frequently in the New Testament. Within the Jewish community there were elders in the Sanhedrin (Luke 22:66; Acts 22:5) and in the synagogue (Luke 7:3). In the Christian community, representatives of the Jerusalem church were called elders. Barnabas and Paul took gifts to Jerusalem and deposited these with "the elders" (Acts 11:30). When problems arose in the church of Antioch, Barnabas and Paul again were designated to travel to Jerusalem to discuss these with "the apostles and the elders" (Acts 15:2). On a later occasion, Paul conferred in Jerusalem with James and "all the elders" (Acts 21:18).

The Pastoral Epistles also feature this title. In 1 Timothy 4:14 reference is made to a council of elders which had appointed Timothy to a particular ministry. In the same epistle an exhortation is made concerning "the elders who rule well." They are to be "considered worthy of double honor, especially those who labor in preaching and teaching" (1 Tim. 5:17). They are to be protected from idle gossip or unfounded accusations, but if they are shown to be living out of harmony with the Christian standard, they are to be publicly rebuked (1 Tim. 5:19-20). The advice which follows here in the text, "Do not be hasty in the laying on of hands" (v. 22), probably refers to the ordination of such elders. Care must be taken to ensure that this solemn office is appropriately filled. The context here is not clear, but it seems unlikely that the elders referred to in this passage form a distinct group of church leaders in addition to the bishops and deacons mentioned in 1 Timothy 3:1-13. It is more probable that the term "elders" could be used as a reference to members of both groups. The passage also suggests that the content of the office varied—some (apparently only some) were involved with preaching and teaching and were to be remunerated more highly than the others.

Elders are also mentioned in the General Epistles. They are to minister to the sick (James 5:14-15). They are not, however, designated to hearing confessions, for that is a community responsibility (James 5:16). Peter, writing to Christians in Asia Minor, addresses an exhortation to the elders and terms himself a "fellow elder." It is clear that Peter sees their function as one of pastoral care with some responsibility for financial matters. And they are to guard against the abuse of their powers (1 Peter 5:1-4).

It is not possible to say with certainty whether bishop and presbyter were two distinct offices in the New Testament period. All that can be inferred is that the offices had considerable overlap. It was in the patristic period of the church's history that each was given a distinct identity. The content of the offices is only vaguely delineated in the New Testament. Although similar titles or offices can be identified in the synagogue, in Pharisaic circles, and in Jewish sectarian life, this does not necessarily imply that the early church patterned its leadership after such models. In this office, as in other areas, the primitive community was innovative. Later Christian communities fashioned the offices to accommodate their own specific needs.

Deacon

The word transliterated as deacon, *diakonos,* is only one of several Greek words referring to service. It does not carry the idea of degradation one would associate with the service of a slave. Rather, it depicts the willing service that springs from a relationship with a master who is well-respected. It is a service of love, as when a person offers hospitality to a guest.

Jesus used the verb *diakoneo* in the analogy in which he described the satisfaction a master feels when he finds that his servants are appropriately prepared for service. What does the master do?

He honors them by insisting that they sit at table while he serves them (Luke 12:35–40). The same word is used to describe the way angels ministered to Jesus during or after his period of testing in the wilderness (Mark 1:13; Matt. 4:11). In the fourth gospel the verb is used in connection with the disciples' attitude toward Jesus, an attitude that brings about the reward of fellowship with God: "If any one serves me, the Father will honor him" (John 12:26). Paul describes himself as a servant (deacon) both of Christ (2 Cor. 11:23) and of the church (Col. 1:24–25). These usages illustrate the two dimensions of service implied in this concept.

Before long, however, the word *diakonos* came to be used in a more technical sense in reference to a special office within the church. Mention is made of "bishops and deacons," as though these two offices were coordinated (see Phil. 1:1). This same conjunction of the two offices is found in the Pastoral Epistles. After the passage dealing with the qualifications of a bishop, the writer gives instruction concerning the kind of people who should be appointed as deacons and deaconesses. They must be men and women who have a serious outlook, who exercise control over their speech, and who are temperate in their personal lives. A married deacon (and, by implication, deaconess) must be successful in the running of his or her own household (1 Tim. 3:8–13).

Concerning the function of a deacon, nothing can be said with much certainty. Because deacons are mentioned alongside bishops, some have suggested that the early church patterned itself after the synagogue structure in which the synagogue ruler was responsible for the conduct of worship and his assistant worked alongside. Perhaps the deacon functioned as assistant to the bishop? If such a parallel existed, then both bishop and deacon would have been responsible only for worship functions because the direction of the synagogue was in the hands of a body of elders.

Because the word *diakonos* was often used in Greek to describe one who waited at table, some have conjectured that in the early church the deacon was responsible for the preparation and serving of the common meal which formed the heart of Christian worship. Also, the early Christians frequently gathered around a table to share in a "love feast" and to commemorate the death of Jesus in the ceremonial eating of bread and drinking of wine. Was this, perhaps, the origin of the need for deacons in the early church?

The tradition that the origin of the diaconate is to be found in the appointment of the seven originated with Irenaeus in the second century C.E. Acts 6:1-6 describes a conflict between the Greek-speaking and the Hebrew-speaking Jewish Christians. The incident concerns the distribution of daily provisions for widows in the various communities and particularly their participation in common meals. The Twelve advised that seven people should be appointed to supervise this duty, so that rather than devoting themselves to "the ministry of tables," they could concern themselves with "the ministry of the word" (Acts 6:2, 4, author's translation). These seven represented for Irenaeus the beginning of an order of church officials differentiated from those responsible for the spiritual welfare of the church. While bishops (the Twelve) should concern themselves with prayer and preaching, deacons (the seven) should be responsible for secular matters such as finances and food.

Since the time of Irenaeus, this has been for many an accepted pattern of church leadership. Deacons are appointed to supervise aid to those in need, the care and upkeep of church property, and administrative concerns, leaving others free to concentrate on more "spiritual" matters. But is this a correct understanding of Acts 6?

Stephen, the first named of the seven, is described as "a man full of faith and of the Holy Spirit" (Acts 6:5). In no sense did he confine himself to the spheres of service mentioned above. He "did great wonders and signs among the people" (Acts 6:8) and spent much of his time debating openly with Jews from Cyrene, Alexandria, Cilicia, and Asia (presumably Greek-speaking Jews). So powerful was his proclamation of the Christian message that "they could not withstand the wisdom and the Spirit with which he spoke" (Acts 6:10). Stephen evidently had perceptive things to say about the relationship between the Christian faith and Judaism, particularly with respect to the temple and the Torah, two central issues. The speech attributed to Stephen in Acts 7 takes up more space than any other speech in this book—an indication that the writer of Acts perceived it as being one of the most significant statements made in those early years. What Stephen said was clearly understood by the Hellenistic Jews: on account of it they put him to death, and he became the first Christian martyr. This reads more like a "ministry of the word" than a "ministry of tables."

Philip was also named among the seven. He, too, carried on a preaching ministry. In Samaria he brought "much joy" to the people through his ministry of preaching, healing, and exorcism. He "preached good news about the kingdom of God and the name of Jesus Christ." Both men and women responded to his preaching and were baptized (Acts 8:4–13). And it was Philip who presented the Christian message to the Ethiopian who, after worshiping in the Jewish temple, was traveling home on the Jerusalem-Gaza road. Philip's exegesis of Isaiah's prophecy led the man to faith in Christ, and Philip baptized him (Acts 8:26–39). Traveling along the coastal regions, Philip preached the Christian message from Azotus to Caesarea (Acts 8:40). Clearly he was concerned with "ministry of the word."

In the light of this information, it is necessary to reevaluate the church's stance on the office of deacon. If the Acts 6 passage is thought to embody the beginnings of the diaconate, then it must be seen in its context. The seven clearly did not confine themselves to administrative duties. They were actively involved in a ministry of preaching, teaching, healing, and baptizing—a ministry identical, it would seem, to that of Paul at a later time. And if the Acts 6 passage is not axiomatic for establishing the role of deacon, then there is little at all in the New Testament concerning the nature of such an office in the early church. If in the past each church structured this office to meet the needs of its own community, then the church of today is free to do likewise.

In 1971, Edward P. Echlin, a Roman Catholic priest and scholar, published a short study on the office of deacon.[8] In this volume he shows how diaconal service gradually declined after its golden age in the pre-Nicene period. Echlin attributes this decline to the rise of sacerdotalism in the third century C.E. and the restrictive ecclesiastical legislation of the early fourth century C.E. Within the Roman Catholic church there developed a confusion of the roles of deacon and priest. In the ensuing struggle for identity, the diaconate receded until it became simply a preliminary step to priesthood. Many centuries later the Council of Trent attempted to restore the diaconal function but without success. It remained temporary, subordinate, and ceremonial. Not until Vatican II, after a lapse of more than a thousand years, was the permanent diaconate restored to the Roman Catholic church.

Echlin sees in this historical perspective a challenge to the church of today. It is within the power of the present-day church to structure or restructure offices in such a way that they fully represent and fully serve the human condition. In the absence of biblical guidelines, as in this instance, no divine law binds the church to any structure of any past generation. Structure that may have been adequate at one time is not necessarily adequate for the present time.

Conclusions

Leadership structure in the early church was diverse. Title and function are not clearly delineated in the New Testament documents. Transitions took place from one leadership pattern to another, sometimes not without conflict and friction. The criterion for leadership was evidently not conformity to other churches. Rather, leadership title and function were geared to the needs of the particular situation. Hans Küng comments that "a frightening gulf separates the church of today from the original constitution of the church."[9] Perhaps a clearer understanding of the original constitution of the church will enable Christians to face the future with more realism and more creativity.

Like the church of yesterday, the church of today must mold its offices to meet the needs of the community. The lethargy that has kept the church in a holding pattern can no longer be tolerated. To excuse it on the basis of "adherence to tradition" is to weakly sidetrack the issue. Tradition is nothing more than a record of the church's efforts to preserve and communicate its treasured message and experience in the most effective way possible. What shame to the present-day church if it rests on the laurels of a past generation and thereby fails its own. The affirmation of the role of women as leaders of Christian communities may be one part of that restructuring. But it is only a part. Perhaps far-reaching changes need to be initiated as a means of creating a new leadership structure which could be more positively geared to the needs of the church of today.

Notes

[1] See Hans Küng, *The Church,* trans., Ray and Rosaleen Ockenden (New York: Sheed & Ward, 1967), p. 345.

[2] For a detailed consideration of these issues, see C. K. Barrett, *The Signs of an Apostle* (Philadelphia: Fortress, 1972).

[3] Raymond Brown, *Priest and Bishop, Biblical Reflections* (New York: Paulist, 1970), pp. 47-86.

[4] Brown, *Priest and Bishop,* pp. 77-78.

[5] Küng, *The Church,* pp. 354-59.

[6] Ibid., p. 358.

[7] Brown, *Priest and Bishop,* pp. 65-69.

[8] Edward P. Echlin, *The Deacon in the Church, Past and Future* (New York: Alba House, 1971).

[9] Küng, *The Church,* p. 413.

THE CHURCH LEADER: A PRIEST?

Historical Background

IN CONSIDERING CHURCH leadership titles and functions from a New Testament perspective in chapter 4, no mention was made of the church leader as a priest. Yet, numerous Christian communities across the world do so designate their leader. What is the origin of the priestly office? And why are Christians divided over this issue?

The priestly function is a characteristic of the period of Israel's history when the tabernacle and the temple were the institutions of Israelite worship. During the wilderness journeyings, when the Hebrew people wandered as nomads in the Sinai peninsula, the presence of Yahweh was symbolized by a special tent pitched in the center of the encampment. The enclosed courtyard surrounding this tent housed an altar, and here animal sacrifices were offered. Heads of families were permitted to enter this courtyard and offer sacrifice, but access to the tent itself was reserved for the priests alone. There they performed religious rites on behalf of the people of Israel.

There are some ambiguities regarding the origins and function of the priestly office. The office was hereditary, but the origins of this custom are not clear. The Hebrew Scriptures speak of a tribe of Levitical priests, but also mention the priesthood of Eli and of Zadok. The function of the priestly office is described in the early sources, but it is not clearly differentiated from the function of the prophetic office. Indeed, the Hebrew word *kohen* (priest) seems to derive from the Arabic word *kahin* (prophet, seer), and to some extent the functions of prophet and priest overlap. The Song of Moses makes reference to three areas of priestly activity (Deut. 33:8-11)—the Levites were to handle the Urim and Thummim, the sacred lot by which Yahweh directed his people; they were to teach the Law of Yahweh; and they were to officiate at the altar of incense and the altar of burnt offering. Sacrifice was thus not the only function or necessarily the most significant function of the priest in the early years of Israelite history. Like the prophet, the priest was a teacher and interpreter of the Law and a mouthpiece through which Yahweh guided his people.

When the Hebrews moved northward into the land of Canaan and became overlords of the large territories of land stretching from the river Nile to the Tigris-Euphrates valley, it was natural that their way of life would become more settled. They built permanent dwellings in place of the movable tents which had previously been their homes. Yahweh, too, it was reasoned, should have a "permanent dwelling," and in the period of the monarchy a splendid temple was built in Jerusalem. Here public sacrifices were offered three times a day and private sacrifices proliferated. Now to a greater extent, the priest was concerned with the ritual offering of sacrifice. Communicating the oracle of God and giving instruction in the Law became less important features of the priestly role. Attempts were made to restrict worship at local shrines and to centralize religious observance in Jerusalem because local sanctuaries could too easily be assimilated to the worship of other gods. The Jerusalem priesthood would preserve the religious rites proper to the worship of Yahweh.

While these developments were taking place, the prophetic tradition was also flourishing in Israel. Schools of prophets came into being, centering around charismatic personalities such as Elijah and Elisha. These prophets were concerned with cultic ritual only when the need arose to challenge its abuse.[1] Rather, the role they assumed was that of proclaimer of the message of Yahweh. The prophets called the people of Israel to social justice, moral purity, and political action in harmony with the divine Law. Boldly they confronted king and peasant alike with the demands of Yahweh, and sometimes they paid for this boldness with their lives.

Unlike the priestly office, the prophetic ministry was not passed down from father to son. It came about as the result of a special call from God, a call which was usually unexpected and sometimes undesired. The prophet was not honored with provisions of food or living expenses. He was not accepted as part of the establishment. But his words were considered of such value that kings would sometimes summon a prophet to "inquire of the Lord" in order to give the country guidance in the conduct of its national affairs.

When Israel's golden age of monarchy came to a close, changes took place in the various forms of religious activity. The temple was destroyed in 586 B.C.E. by the invading Babylonians, and its ritual was therefore suspended. Exiled in the Tigris-Euphrates valley, the Hebrew people could only remember with longing the city of David and the temple of Solomon. Away from the holy place, no sacrifice could be offered. Tenaciously the Hebrews held onto what was left of their religious tradition and found in it their riches—the transmission of the sacred writings, the practice of circumcision, and the observance of the Sabbath rest recalling them to the worship of Yahweh in song and in prayer. The synagogue communities which came into being at this time needed no priest because sacrifice formed no part of their worship. But from time to time attempts were made by returning exiles to rebuild the temple and reestablish its cultus.

Ironically, it was Herod the Great, a much disliked "foreign" despot who restored to the temple some of its former glory (18 B.C.E.). The priestly ritual once more had meaning. Twenty-four courses of priests each served in the temple one week at a time, twice a year. When not on duty, they returned to their wives and families and pursued a secular calling. The figure of the high priest emerged around this time. The high priest was the president of the Sanhedrin, the Jewish council, and was responsible for oversight of the temple ritual.

The New Testament refers frequently to "priests and Levites," indicating that different classes of priests existed within the framework of the temple organization. The Levites were probably descendants of the earlier rural priests and seem to have been responsible for more lowly temple duties and for the music which accompanied worship. They did not have access to the altar or the sanctuary.[2] Scribes are also referred to in the New Testament alongside the priests. In the intertestamental period the scribes had become established as the experts in the Jewish Law. They were the scholars who could provide knowledge of this Law and insight concerning its meaning and application. They were now partners with the priests and respected leaders of the people. Unhappily, as a result of political intrigue, the priests of this period were sometimes more the pawns of the state than the ministers of God.

Hoping one day for the restoration of a "pure priesthood," the Qumran community withdrew into the Judean desert to prepare itself for a dramatic return to the scene of action. They at least would be ritually clean and in a state of spiritual submission to God, ready for his service. But the dream of the Qumran covenanters was not to be realized. In 66 C.E. the Jews rebelled against Rome and in 70 C.E. the invading army of Titus razed the temple. The holy place was defiled, and sacrifice could no more be offered within the temple precincts.

The Bar-Cochba uprising against the Romans in 132 C.E. was glorious but short-lived. Within three years the rebellion was suppressed, and the Jewish people were denied entry to their once holy city. Jerusalem became a Roman colony, and its name was changed to Colonia Aelia Capitolina in honor of the Roman god Jupiter. From that age to this there has been no sacrificial cultus within the mainstream of Judaism. Instead of the priest, the scribe became the all-important religious figure and the true center of the community. The Torah which he expounded became the focus of Israelite thought. Temple, sacrifice, and priest no longer feature in the expression of Jewish worship.

The prophetic voice was also silenced in Israel. The age of the great writing prophets—Amos, Hosea, Isaiah, Jeremiah, Ezekiel, and others—passed away, though their works were carefully copied and preserved for future generations. Haggai, Zechariah, and Malachi were the last of these great spokesmen for God, and their activity is generally assigned to the sixth and fifth centuries B.C.E. After that came a great silence, unbroken until the voice of John the Baptist sounded in the Judean desert in the first century C.E. In true prophetic tradition John called the people to repentance. Honesty, justice, and compassion were to be the guidelines for social action. The sovereignty of God was to be recognized. And then came Jesus, and a new community was born.

New Testament Documents

The community of Jesus came into being within the shadow of the temple walls. Viewing itself as Israel renewed, its twelve apostles symbolically patterning the twelve tribes of Israel, it would have been natural for this community to model its leadership structure on that of the Jewish temple. But it did not do so. Concerning leadership "set apart" specifically for ceremonial observance the New Testament is silent.

Nor did the leadership style in the Christian community parallel leadership concepts in the political arena. In a context in which two apostles were aspiring to positions of honor, Jesus gave some clear guidelines concerning the nature of the leadership function in his community:

> "You know that those who are supposed to rule over the Gentiles lord it over them, and their great men exercise authority over them. But it shall not be so among you; but whoever

would be great among you must be your servant, and whoever would be first among you must be slave of all" (Mark 10:42-44).

The idea of ruling over or exercising authority over is foreign to the concept of leadership expressed here by Jesus.[3] Rather, the leader is to be a servant *(diakonos),* indeed a slave *(doulos).* "The leader," Luke records, must become "as one who serves" (Luke 22:26). Jesus himself epitomized this in his relationship with his disciples —"I am among you as one who serves" (Luke 22:27), and he demonstrated it profoundly when he girded himself with a cloth and washed the disciples' feet, assuming the common role of the house servant (John 13:4-5, 12-17). But service in this context is more than being prepared to do menial tasks for another person. It involves an orientation of life in which the total person is at the disposition of another and is promoting his or her good—"The Son of man came not to be served but to serve, and to give his life as a ransom for many" (Matt. 20:28).

Nor did the emerging leaders of the Christian community take Pharisaic leadership as a model for their own. The Pharisees wore distinctive clothing which identified them as religious people. Some rejoiced in the consequent honor ascribed to them and the feeling of superiority which resulted from this. Jesus said of these:

> "They love the place of honor at feasts and the best seats in the synagogues, and salutations in the market places, and being called rabbi by men" (Matt. 23:6-7).

Such an assumption of dignity did not foster the cause of discipleship to which Jesus was committed.

> "But you are not to be called rabbi, for you have one teacher, and you are all brethren. And call no man your father on earth, for you have one Father, who is in heaven. Neither be called masters, for you have one master, the Christ. He who is greatest among you shall be your servant" (Matt. 23:8-11).

Why, then, in some circles is the Christian leader spoken of as priest? The New Testament is not silent about priesthood. Jesus affirmed the authority of the priest when he commanded a leper to present himself to a priest to be officially declared clean (Matt. 8:4). And although the story of the Good Samaritan clearly implies a criticism of the priesthood (Luke 10:31), this is a mild criticism in comparison with that given by the ancient prophets (see Amos 5:21-24). In Acts we read that "a great many of the priests were obedient to the faith" (Acts 6:7). There is, however, little evidence that Jesus designated himself as a priest, or that he so designated his disciples.

The writers of the Gospels certainly have little to say about the priesthood of Christ. Luke, in his nativity narratives, draws a distinction between the tribal ancestry of John the Baptist and that of Jesus. John was the son of "a priest named Zechariah" who was married to "a wife of the daughters of Aaron" (Luke 1:5). It was while Zechariah was serving as priest in the Jerusalem temple that he was told of the imminent birth of a special child—his own child, John. Jesus was born to a family claiming descent from the tribe of Judah, directly through the line of kingship (Luke 3:23-38). Mary is described as a "kinswoman" of Elizabeth, the wife of Zechariah, and could therefore be assumed to have had family connections with the priestly tribe of Aaron, although the nature of these is not known (Luke 1:36). Yet Luke, in spite of his considerable emphasis on the temple, gives no hint in his gospel that Jesus was thought of in terms of priesthood.

The priesthood of Christ is, however, featured prominently in the letter to the Hebrews. Here Jesus is described not as priest but as the "high priest of our confession" (Heb. 3:1). However, his high priesthood is different from that of the high priests who were descended from Levi. In the first place (and this is perhaps the most significant point for this present consideration), Christ, like Melchizedek of old, has no successor—"He holds his priesthood permanently, because he continues for ever" (Heb. 7:24). In the second place, Christ combines in his own person both priest and sacrifice (Heb. 9:11-12). Finally, unlike the sacrifice of the ancient cultus, the sacrifice made by Christ needs no repetition—"Nor was it to offer himself repeatedly . . . for then he would have had to suffer repeatedly" (Heb. 9:25–26). The sacrifice of Christ, offered only once, is complete and final:

> When Christ had offered for all time a single sacrifice for sins, he sat down at the right hand of God, then to wait until his enemies should be made a stool for his feet. For by a single offering he has perfected for all time those who are sanctified (Heb. 10:12–14).

The fact that Christ is seated emphasizes that he has no need, like the Levitical priests, to stand daily offering continual sacrifice. The offering of himself was a once-for-all-time event. The present ministry of Christ is not a ministry of sacrifice but a ministry of intercession (Heb. 7:25).

Perhaps, in presenting the work of Christ in this perspective, the writer of Hebrews was attempting to come to terms with the enforced ending of the sacrificial ministry of priests in the Jerusalem temple (70 C.E.). What appeared to be an act of oppression by the Romans could be interpreted as an act of God. There was no need of the "shadow" (the temple cultus) because the "reality" (the sacrifice of Christ) had been manifested. The Christian Jew did not need to lament the cessation of animal sacrifice in the Jerusalem temple; one perfect and all-sufficient sacrifice had been offered.

Among the other New Testament passages which have bearing on this issue, 1 Peter 2:9 is significant. Addressing the entire Christian community, the writer states, "You are a chosen race, a royal priesthood, a holy nation, God's own people." So the Christian community as a whole is spoken of in terms of a priesthood; as such, it must be concerned to "offer spiritual sacrifices acceptable to God" (1 Peter 2:5).

The same thought is expressed in Revelation 1:6, where Christ is described as the one who has "made us a kingdom, priests to his God and Father" (cf. Rev. 5:10). Such expressions imply that each Christian is set apart for sacred ministry; they do not foreshadow the reintroduction of a sacrificial cult or a hierarchy of leadership. It is notable that in his vision of the New Jerusalem, the writer of Revelation saw no temple in the city (Rev. 21:22), although the city clearly portrayed the perfection of the age to come. The temple symbolized the presence of God among his people. But there is no need for the symbol when the reality is experienced (Rev. 21:3).

Thus the New Testament speaks of the Christian community as a whole in terms of a "priesthood" and of Christ in terms of a "high priest." All who believe are "a holy priesthood," and jointly they offer to God "spiritual sacrifices." As "high priest," Christ has offered the perfect sacrifice which need never be repeated. Respecting this perspective, Protestant churches have generally avoided the use of the term *priest* to designate their leadership. The Roman Catholic church, however, does so designate its leaders. The reasons for this must be examined.[4]

Early Church History

It is the practice of the Roman Catholic church to appoint bishops over certain geographical areas. These men are thought to be successors to the apostles, although they are not, like the apostles, itinerant evangelists, but supervisory agents within the church structure. They accept responsibility for the spiritual welfare of the churches within their territory. These churches are in turn supervised by local ministers, or priests. It is the conviction of Roman Catholic theologians that the ministerial priesthood differs from the priesthood shared by all the baptized, not only in degree but also in essence.

This concept gained acceptance only gradually in the early centuries of the Christian Era. Traces of its development can be found in the Didache, a document dating from the early second century. The Didache makes a simple comparison between the prophets of the Christian Era and the high priests of Judaism, suggesting that like the priests these spiritual leaders should be provided with food. "Take all the first fruits of the winepress and of the harvest, of the cattle and of the sheep, and give them to the prophets, for they are your high priests" (Did. 13:3, in *FC*, 1:182).

Coming from the same time period, the letters of Ignatius speak frequently of three categories of church leadership—bishop, priest, and deacon. "Let all follow the bishop as Jesus Christ did the Father, and the priests, as you would the Apostles. Reverence the deacons as you would the command of God" ("To Smyrnaens," 8, in *FC*, 1:121). Of these, the bishop is the most highly honored. Nothing, according to Ignatius, must be done in the church without his approval, in particular the celebration of the eucharist and of baptism. The longer recension (which is probably spurious) of the letter of Ignatius to Smyrna describes the bishop as a high priest, "who bears the image of God—of God inasmuch as he is a ruler, and of Christ, in his capacity of a priest." His position is indeed an exalted one. "Nor is there any one in the Church greater than the bishop, who ministers as a priest to God for the salvation of the whole world" ("To Smyrnaens," 9, in *ANF*, 1:90).

Tertullian, writing in the third century C.E., also refers to the bishop as the chief priest *(summus sacerdos)* and to the presbyters as priests ("On Baptism," 17, in *ANF*, 3:677). And in the fourth century C.E., the church historian Eusebius, addressing an assembly of clergy, greets them as "friends and priests of God who are clothed with the holy robe and the heavenly crown of glory, the inspired unction and the priestly raiment of the Holy Spirit" (Ecc. Hist. 10:4, 2, in *FC*, 29:244).

In this early period, the designation of the church minister as priest speaks of his function rather than of any particular priestly dignity. Tertullian indicates that bishops have the right to baptize new converts, but it is clear that he does not regard this as an exclusive right. Presbyters and deacons may also baptize—even laymen may baptize as the need arises. The idea of sacerdotal character is clearly ruled out. The bishop was chosen by all and ordained by all and acted simply as a representative of the people.[5]

The natural concomitant of the concept of the church leader as a priest is that of the church as a temple and the table from which the bread and wine are served as an altar. Judaizing tendencies are discernible in many strata of the early Christian tradition, and this is an example of such. At first it was a matter of analogy only. Ignatius exhorted the Magnesians, "Hasten all of you together as to one temple of God, to one altar, to Jesus Christ alone" ("To the Magnesians," 7, in *FC*, 1:98). It was essential that the Christian community assemble for worship, its spiritual sustenance. "If a person is not inside the sanctuary he is deprived of the Bread" ("To the Ephesians," 5, in *FC*, 1:89). Being under the sphere of influence of the bishops, priests, and deacons was regarded as being "within the sanctuary." Here was purity. Outside was only impurity ("To the Trallians," 7, in *FC*, 1:104).

Gradually a change came about in the understanding of the eucharist. Rather than being a memorial meal conducted in a domestic setting, it became more specifically a sacrifice performed at an altar. In the Didache the church is instructed:

> On the Lord's day, after you have come together, break bread and offer the Eucharist, having first confessed your offences, so that your sacrifice may be pure. . . . For it was said by the Lord: "In every place and time let there be offered to me a clean sacrifice, because I am the great king"; and also: "and my name is wonderful among the Gentiles" (Did. 14:1, 3, in *FC*, 1:182).

The reference here is to the writings of the prophet Malachi:

> For from the rising of the sun to its setting my name is great among the nations, and in every place incense is offered to my name, and a pure offering; for my name is great among the nations, says the Lord of hosts (Mal. 1:11).

This idea of a perpetual offering of sacrifice at all times and in all places was seen to be fulfilled in the perpetual "offering" of the eucharist. Justin Martyr argued that the God of the Christians "has no need of streams of blood and libations and incense" ("First Apology," 13, in *ANF*, 1:166) and that instead he demands only that his community offer to him spiritual sacrifices of prayer and thanksgiving. Nevertheless, the table of the Lord came to be spoken of as an "altar" and the bread and wine as an "offering." Clement of Rome speaks of the bishops as those who have "blamelessly and in holiness offered up sacrifice" ("Letter to the Corinthians," 44:4, in *FC*, 1:44). This concept was to hold sway for many years to come.

From the mid-fourth century onward a change gradually took place in the manner of appointing church leaders and in the popular understanding of the priestly office. A distinction developed between the clergy and the laity. Once the term *laity* had referred to the whole people of God; now it was used to describe those Christians who did not hold official church office. Gradually it was decreed that only the clergy had the right to appoint bishops, and only bishops had the right to appoint priests.

By the time of Augustine, the Latin church had developed a theology of ordination in which the rite was understood as a sacrament. It conferred on the recipient a definite "imprint" or "character" which empowered him to perform priestly duties. Even if he should become an apostate, this character would still remain with him. It was independent of his own state of devotion to Christ. Thus, Augustine argued, any priestly act such a person performs is to be considered valid irrespective of his commitment to the faith.[6] Gradually the Latin church withdrew from the laity the privilege of presiding at the eucharist and of granting absolution after the hearing of confessions, and only in exceptional circumstances might the lay person perform the rite of baptism. Henceforth these areas were to be the prerogative of the priest.

The Eastern church, while assimilating some of these ideas from the Latin church, maintained certain distinctions. Significant to the Eastern church was the relationship between the personal life of the priest and the holy office he performed. Earlier the Didache had warned: "Not everyone who speaks in the spirit is a prophet, but only if he follows the conduct of the Lord" (Did. 11:8, in *FC*, 1:181); and Irenaeus had exhorted: "Adhere to those . . . who, together with the order of priesthood *(presbyterii ordine),* display sound speech and blameless conduct" ("Against Heresies," 26:4, in *ANF,* 1:497). The Eastern church similarly insisted that, as a leader and example, the priest must live a life of greater dedication than that of the ordinary Christian. This would not come about automatically as a result of his ordination. If after ordination there was no transformation of the priest's inner life resulting in holy and humble service, then his priesthood was open to question. This perspective is closely aligned with that of primitive Christianity.[7]

The Issue in the Roman Catholic Church Today

The sacramental concept of priesthood has been maintained by the Latin church up to the present day. Recently some Roman Catholic scholars have attempted to demonstrate that this is not simply a result of theological development but is intrinsic to the biblical documents themselves. Andre Feuillet addresses himself to significant issues: Was Christ a priest? Did he think of himself in priestly terms? Were the apostles constituted priests by Christ? Is the priesthood of church leaders different in essence from that of the church as a whole?[8]

Feuillet maintains that the letter to the Hebrews is not the only biblical source of information on the priesthood of Christ. He argues that there is evidence in the Gospels to suggest that Psalm 110 exercised considerable influence on Jesus' understanding of his own person. The opening verse of this psalm—"Sit at my right hand, till I make your enemies your footstool"—has reference to royal dignity. Although not quoted in the Gospels, verse 4 of this psalm links the idea of royal dignity with that of priesthood: "You are a priest for ever after the order of Melchizedek." Feuillet also sees significance in the fact that Isaiah 53 forms a strong background to the passion narrative. In this "servant song" there is a fusing of the priestly role (the offering of sacrifice, Isa. 53:4–5) with that of the prophet (intercessory prayer, 53:12). As Ezekiel was both prophet and priest, so Christ fulfilled a dual role.

Feuillet gives great importance to the Johannine presentation of the work of Christ. He interprets the account of the footwashing (John 13:3-14) as a ritual cleansing in preparation for priesthood; the lengthy prayer of Jesus in John 17 he sees as a consecration of Jesus and his disciples: ("I consecrate myself, that they also may be consecrated in truth," John 17:19); and the resurrection narrative in which Jesus breathed on the disciples and said, "Receive the Holy Spirit" (John 20:22) he understands as referring to their ordination as priests. From this time onward they have power to forgive sins.[9]

Even though scholars such as Feuillet feel confident that there is in the New Testament a foreshadowing of the concept of the church leader as a priest, there are many Roman Catholic scholars and lay people who are questioning the appropriateness of this designation. In his address to the Roman clergy on 20 February 1971,[10] Pope Paul VI addressed himself to this issue. He voiced a question frequently asked today: "Is the existence of a priesthood really justified in the economy of the New Testament?"[11] The New Testament teaches, the pontiff observed, that the Levitical priesthood is finished and can never be reinstated because its raison d'être has ceased (Heb. 10:12-18). The New Testament presents Christ as the one and only mediator between God and men (1 Tim. 2:5). Every Christian is a member of the royal priesthood established by Christ (1 Peter 2:9), and the true worship of the community is to be offered not through any temple ritual but "in spirit and truth" (John 4:21-24). The pontiff exhorted the clergy to pray, hope, and work toward the renewal of a genuine concept of church leadership which would respond to the needs of today's world.

The results of some of that "work" are reflected in the documents which have emerged from Vatican II.[12] In essentials, however, there is little change from the concepts held from the time of Augustine. The hierarchical structure of the church is reaffirmed, with a line of authority passing from Christ through the apostles and bishops to the priests. Priests are said to be "signed with a special character" and are able to "act in the person of Christ."

They have the power to offer sacrifice. The eucharist is regarded as the most significant act of Christian worship and the focal point of the priestly ministry. It is spoken of as a sacrifice which is offered daily, and in presiding at this the priest is performing an act in which a "divine victim" is offered to God. Teaching such as this clearly communicates the idea of an often-repeated sacrifice.

Pope John Paul II, in his "Letter to all the Priests of the Church," Holy Thursday, 1979,[13] endorses these viewpoints. The Sacrament of Orders confers on the recipient a priesthood which differs from that of other believers in degree and in essence. It is not the community which selects and appoints priests; rather, it is Christ who calls and enables some "to be ministers of his own sacramental sacrifice." *In persona Christi* the priest "effects the Eucharistic Sacrifice and offers it to God in the name of all the people" (*Lumen Gentium,* 10). To this priesthood is granted the power of forming and governing the church.

No group of people is more conscious of the dilemmas posed by these issues than that group they most affect, namely Roman Catholic priests and theologians. Hans Küng, writing prior to Vatican II, draws out the implications of the concept of the "priesthood of all believers."[14] This, he maintains, has concrete reality even in formal worship. Each Christian has direct access to God and is free to offer to God spiritual sacrifices of prayer, praise, penitence, kindness, and love. The command to preach the word is given to all Christians, not to a select few. And the commands of Jesus relating to Baptism, the eucharist, and absolution were given to all his disciples, not just to the Twelve. There is no reason, then, to reserve to the clergy the right to officiate at these observances.

In the same way, the entire community of faith is given the task of acting as mediator between God and the world—this is not an exclusive function of selected members of the community. Küng sees nothing wrong in calling the church leader "priest." All Christians are priests, and the title is therefore appropriate. But to view such a person as priest in an exclusive sense, Küng maintains, is contrary to the teachings of the New Testament. The decrees of Vatican II did not redress this balance.

The extent to which the eucharist may be regarded as a sacrifice is also open to debate. Raymond Brown maintains that the sacrifices referred to in the New Testament are those involving a certain manner of life; they are not ritual offerings. In New Testament times the eucharist was not thought of as a sacrifice and had no specific association with the idea of priesthood. "There is no proof," Brown writes, "that the Christian communities who broke the eucharistic bread after the resurrection would have thought that they were offering sacrifice."[15] Rather, the eucharist was a communal meal which took place in a domestic environment. The role of presiding at its celebration was "but one of many spiritual ministries, some of which are far more prominent in the pages of Scripture."[16] Brown maintains that other ministries have more significance in an understanding of the role of a priest than does the celebration of the eucharist.[17]

Charles R. Meyer takes issue with the concept of the priest as a "man apart."[18] Paul, apostle par excellence, worked at a trade during the week and preached and pastored in his spare time (Acts 18:1–4). Most of the other apostles were married (1 Cor. 9:5). Prior to the Council of Trent (1563 C.E.) it was usual for church leaders to be very much a part of secular society, working in government posts or in agriculture, or serving in the military. The education these people acquired was not always exclusively in theology. Meyer questions the precedents for a person being devoted full-time to church leadership. The Council of Carthage (429 C.E.) insisted that "a cleric must support himself by learning some trade." It was semi-Pelagian heretics who first began teaching that clergy should not be involved in manual work.

Meyer appeals to the church to consider the past when planning for the future. "It is unconscionable," he writes, "in an institution dedicated to the preservation of tradition to be uninformed about that tradition."[19] The church as a community possesses the priestly charism. An individual may partake of this in a special way if he is seen by the community to have intelligence, leadership potential, and saintliness of life which comes from a special operation of the Holy Spirit. These graces are not conferred by ordination. Ordination is a recognition of the presence of these graces. It is the church's way of empowering a member to become an official representative. The priest then becomes an ambassador for the church and may act in such capacity.

Women and Priesthood

The evolution of the concept of the church leader as priest has had far-reaching consequences in the attitude of the church toward women and church leadership. Whereas in the Hebrew Scriptures there are precedents for women fulfilling the prophetic ministry, there are no precedents for women fulfilling the role of priest. Indeed, women generally were excluded from the sanctuary. The reason usually given for this in the patristic literature is that menstruation is an "uncleanness" which disqualifies a woman from priestly service. This idea is reflected also in an apocryphal document, the *Protevangelium of James*, which describes the childhood of Mary. According to this document, Mary was devoted to God from the time of her conception and at the age of three was brought to the temple and given over to the care of the priests. All went well until Mary began to mature; then the priests faced a dilemma.

> When [Mary] was twelve years old, there took place a council of the priests, saying: "Behold, Mary has become twelve years old in the temple of the Lord. What shall we do with her, that she may not pollute the temple of the Lord?"[20]

No longer could the holy sanctuary house the child who had become a woman. A husband must be found for her, and she must be taken to his home. The patristic literature reflects a similar sentiment: those regulations which permit women to exercise leadership functions in the church state that the women must be of an age when the menstrual flow has ceased.

None of this can be adduced very clearly from the regulations concerning the appointment of priests in the Hebrew Scriptures. It is certainly true that any emission from the body was considered to be a defilement, and this included the woman's discharge of blood (Lev. 15:19-24). After the birth of a child a woman had to absent herself from the religious center for a lengthy period of time and then offer sacrifice before she could be accounted ritually clean (Lev. 12:1-8). But the emission of semen by the male was also a defilement and disqualified him from officiating in the holy place. As a result, it became customary for priests to abstain from sexual intercourse for the duration of their priestly service. However, it was recognized that an emission of semen could take place at times other than that of copulation, and this was equally a defilement (Lev. 15:16-18). Indeed, the male emission of semen can occur with more frequency and less predictability than the menstrual flow in a woman. As priestly service was, in any case, intermittent, it is not clear why menstruation in itself would disqualify a woman from priesthood. It seems more likely that the reason for an all-male priesthood can be traced to cultural pressures: the patriarchal orientation of social life, or perhaps the necessary resistance to the fertility cults of the surrounding peoples.

Whatever the reason, the fact remains that there is no precedent for women priests in Israelite tradition. Therefore, once the church leader was conceived in terms of a priest, a strong argument arose in favor of excluding women from this office.

The influence of this concept is strongly present in the twentieth century both within and without the ranks of Roman Catholicism. Often it takes the form of debate concerning the priestly role of representing God to his people. It is often assumed that God is male and that the priest, in order to preserve the visual sign or symbolism, must also be male. That such an idea is theologically untenable is now generally acknowledged.[21]

A similar line of reasoning is pursued in the Vatican II Declaration, *Inter Insigniores*. Here it is argued that in consecrating the

65076

eucharist the priest acts *"in persona Christi,* taking the role of Christ to the point of being his very image." It is argued that "there would not be this 'natural resemblance' which must exist between Christ and his minister if the role of Christ were not taken by a man."[22]

There are at least two problems arising from this viewpoint. One problem is that the focal point of the eucharist should be the bread and the wine, not the one who officiates at the celebration. To transfer the focus from the elements which symbolize the body and blood of Jesus to the person who blesses and distributes the food is to weaken the significance of the celebration. The meaning of the eucharist is found in the fact that each member of the community shares equally in the elements and thus in Christ.

The second problem relates to "natural resemblance." That Christ was born male is not disputed. The question is whether or not a woman may fully represent Christ. By any interpretation of New Testament theology, the answer would be positive. Women and men participate equally in the divine graces. The exhortation "that Christ may dwell in your hearts through faith" and "that you may be filled with all the fulness of God" (Eph. 3:17, 19) is addressed to women as well as to men. When speaking of spiritual realities, distinctions of sex become insignificant (Gal. 3:28). There is an equality transcending any culturally bound distinctions. So the "natural resemblance" has reference only to the fact that if a church congregation sees a male body, it is more particularly reminded of Christ. The "sign," these people are suggesting, must not simply be a human body (incarnation), but a male body. The logical corollary would be that in every other area of Christian living the male may more perfectly represent Christ, again an idea foreign to New Testament teaching.

If, in fact, the issue is based on symbolic resemblance, another point to bear in mind is that the person who officiates at the eucharist is acting also in the place of the church. It was the disciples who were instructed, "Do this in remembrance of me" (1 Cor. 11:24). On behalf of the community the leader blesses and distributes the bread and the wine so that together they may "proclaim the Lord's death until he comes" (1 Cor. 11:26). As the church is frequently referred to as the "bride" of Christ (2 Cor. 11:2; Rev. 21:2; et al.), it seems equally fitting that she be represented by a woman.

It is not only in the eucharist that this dual symbolism is apparent. The church leader, like the prophets and priests of old, represents God to the community and the community to God. In liturgical service this is symbolized by the positioning of the leader between the altar and the congregation so that the leader may face first one and then the other.[23] On behalf of the people, the leader prays to God; on behalf of God, the leader exhorts the people. Granted this dual role, there is no logical reason why a woman could not provide as acceptable a symbol as a man, given the biblical teaching of the church as a bride and the common understanding that God is, in fact, neither male nor female.

Conclusions

Although there is no biblical precedent for an understanding of the church leader as priest, the analogy proved to be an attractive one. A transition came about: the church leader was no longer simply like a priest but was in fact consecrated a priest. As such, the leader moved from the ranks of the laity into a special class set apart from Christians in general. Because there was no precedent for the appointment of women priests in Judaism, women, who had up to this time exercised leadership positions in the church, were excluded from the upper ranks of the gradually developing hierarchy. The eucharist was interpreted in terms of a sacrifice, and ritual purity was to be maintained by those who served at the holy altar. Women were "defiled" by menstruation and were to keep separate from the sacred focus of the church's offering.

The question the church of today must consider is to what extent this development is meaningful. Does the concept of the church leader as a priest harmonize with the biblical teaching on church leadership? Can it be shown that the historical development of this tradition has been healthy? And does such a concept of leadership meet the specific needs of the church of the twentieth century?

While the church should not underestimate the importance of mystery and transcendence in the Christian faith and way of life, the realistic needs of a church community demand a leadership structure which is closely geared to the everyday life of its people. Ideally, a church leader is one whose way of life may be emulated by each member of the congregation. The church is not looking for a model of perfection or a token Christian who may be assigned as a light to the community in general. Rather, it is looking for a representative who will organize and coordinate its efforts to grow to spiritual maturity. The church must therefore demonstrate a willingness to sever itself from the accretions of former times if these accretions are no longer of value in serving the needs of the community of the present. And the church must be courageous enough to create if necessary a new leadership structure, one which is consistent with the teaching of Scripture and geared positively to the situation in which the church finds itself today.

Notes

[1] The word "cultus" (adj., "cultic") is used in this chapter to refer to the ritual institutions of Israelite worship up to and including the period of the Second Temple (first century C.E.).

[2] See Ezekiel 44:9-16.

[3] See 1 Peter 5:3: "not . . . domineering over those in your charge but being examples."

[4] For a Protestant perspective on this subject, see Gerhard Ebeling, *The Word of God and Tradition* (Philadelphia: Fortress, 1968; first published in Göttingen, 1964).

[5] See Hans von Campenhausen, *Tradition and Life in the Church,* trans. A. V. Littledale (London: Collins, 1968), pp. 217-23.

[6] Ibid., p. 230. Von Campenhausen comments that this is strongly suggestive of magic and is cruder than concepts found in any non-Christian priesthood. See also p. 224.

[7] Ibid., pp. 226-30.

[8] Andre Feuillet, *The Priesthood of Christ and His Ministries,* trans. Matthew J. O'Connell (New York: Doubleday, 1975).

[9]In the Synoptics, this power is granted also to the Christian community as a whole. See Matthew 18:18-20.

[10]*The Teachings of Pope Paul VI, 1971* (Washington, D.C.: U.S. Catholic Conference Publications Office, 1972), pp. 223-30.

[11]Ibid., p. 224.

[12]See "Decree on the Ministry and Life of Priests," in *Vatican Council II,* ed. A. Flannery (New York: Costello, 1975), pp. 863-902.

[13]*L'Osservatore Romano* N 16 (577), April 17, 1979.

[14]Hans Küng, *The Church,* trans. Ray and Rosaleen Ockenden (New York: Sheed & Ward, 1967), pp. 363-87.

[15]Raymond Brown, *Priest and Bishop* (New York: Paulist, 1970), p. 16.

[16]Ibid., p. 20.

[17]For the views of Hans Küng and Raymond Brown on the apostolic succession, see chapter 4 of this volume.

[18]Charles R. Meyer, *Man of God* (New York: Doubleday, 1974).

[19]Ibid., p. 34.

[20]Edgar Hennecke, *New Testament Apocrypha,* trans. R. McLachlan Wilson (Philadelphia: Westminster, 1963), 1:378.

[21]See W. Phipps, "The Sex of God," *Journal of Ecumenical Studies* (1979) 16:3; pp. 515-517.

[22]*The Order of Priesthood* (Huntington, Ind.: Our Sunday Visitor, 1978), p. 12. This volume contains the text of the Declaration and the official commentaries on it.

[23]In Roman Catholic churches designed (or remodeled) since Vatican II, the leader stands behind the altar facing the congregation. This has interesting theological implications. It reinforces the concept of the priest as the representative of God and it lessens the priest's identity with the people, thus widening the gap between laity and priesthood.

CELIBACY AND
MINISTRY

WIDE IS THE chasm which separates the scriptural injunction, "a bishop must be the husband of one wife" (1 Tim. 3:2), from the Vatican II ruling, "public commitment to holy celibacy . . . is to precede ordination."[1] How did such a transition come about? The answer to this question lies tangled in traditions which evolved during the first thousand years of the church's history.

One simple explanation of that transition may be found in the developing concept of the church leader as a priest. As a priest, the church leader must maintain priestly purity for the duration of his term of office. In the Herodian temple period, priests were called on to officiate for sessions of about one week twice a year. During this time they were required to abstain from sexual intercourse because the bodily emissions this produced were considered a defilement.[2] But the church leader is called to assume a perpetual office. He must be ready at all times to perform priestly acts, and for this reason he must abstain entirely from sexual intercourse. Therefore, he must remain unmarried.

The concept of the church leader as priest and as celibate had far-reaching implications for women. In the previous chapter it was shown that women were excluded from the priestly office because there was no precedent in Judaism for women priests. But when some branches of the church required not only that priests be male but also that they be celibate, women were moved even further from the pulse of the church's life, for the church leader must be a man who had no intimate contact with a woman.

In order to overcome the problems and temptations inherent in the requirement of celibacy, certain steps had to be taken. A priest must not cultivate friendships with women, for a friendship could easily develop into a romantic attachment which might lead to a denial of priestly vows. For mutual encouragement and support priests must rely on other priests, living in an all-male community and drawing strength from their peers. Women could enter such houses as servants to prepare and serve food, to perform janitorial duties, or to attend to laundry, but they could not associate as equals, as confidants, or as co-workers.

This all-male leadership structured itself into a self-perpetuating hierarchy, excluding women from the decision-making process at all levels. Doctrine was developed and promulgated, policies were established, legislation was passed—all without the active participation of 50 percent of the church's membership. The church thus presented to the world a powerful statement concerning the value of women and their place within the Christian community. Women were to be followers, not leaders. Their gifts were not to be utilized in the upper levels of the church's life, but only in the lower levels of menial service. They must keep a certain distance from the holy sanctuary to avoid bringing defilement on it. On a personal level, their very presence was to be considered a source of temptation to a priest. If he "sinned" in this respect, women were guilty of using their sexual powers to seduce him from his holy calling. To be a woman was in many ways to be an inferior person.

New Testament Background

There is very little material in the New Testament on the subject of celibacy. It appears that nearly all the apostles were married and that the brothers of Jesus who later became leaders in the early church were also married. Paul writes that among that group only he and Barnabas chose to remain single (1 Cor. 9:5). There were women who traveled with Jesus and his disciples, and it is likely that this group included some of the wives (Luke 8:1–3). In any case, wives of a slightly later period did accompany their husbands when they were involved in itinerant ministries, as Paul mentions in 1 Corinthians 9:5. Why, then, this growing trend toward celibacy?

Of the biblical reasons adduced, the most significant one seems to be that Jesus was unmarried and that the church leader wished to identify with Jesus as closely as possible. However, the fact that Jesus was unmarried was unusual by Jewish standards.[3] It was the responsibility of a Jewish father to provide his son with three things—circumcision, a knowledge of Torah, and a wife. It may well have been the unique nature of his calling that led Jesus to forego marriage.

One of the few sayings of Jesus which have bearing on this issue is that concerning "eunuchs." The context of the saying deals with marriage and divorce and the value of children. Jesus makes a clear statement against divorce—so clear that the disciples observe that if the standard is so strict, it might indeed be wiser not to marry! Jesus' response to such a sentiment is guarded:

> "Not all men can receive this precept, but only those to whom it is given. For there are eunuchs who have been so from birth, and there are eunuchs who have been made eunuchs by men, and there are eunuchs who have made themselves eunuchs for the sake of the kingdom of heaven" (Matt. 19:11–12).

The question is, Who are those "to whom it is given" to receive this statement? And, as the first two situations are usually not a matter of choice, the focus of attention is on the third, namely, those "who have made themselves eunuchs for the sake of the kingdom of heaven."

It is generally understood that this third category concerns those who have chosen to deny themselves sexual fulfillment in order to promote the kingdom of God on earth. This did not apply to Jesus' disciples because most of them were, it seems, married. However, Peter's later statement, "Lo, we have left everything and followed you" (Matt. 19:27), is sometimes taken to imply that Peter at least left his wife when traveling with Jesus during his public ministry. In the light of 1 Corinthians 9:5 it would seem that if this was so, it was a temporary arrangement rather than a permanent one. Nevertheless, in the patristic period it was used to encourage a married man who wanted to become a priest to put away his wife and live separately from her forever. Although this is in direct contradiction to the teaching of Jesus that "what therefore God has joined together, let no man put asunder" (Matt. 19:6), it became a widespread practice in the Roman Catholic church.

Another saying of Jesus on this issue is in the context of the resurrection life. "When [people] rise from the dead, they neither marry nor are given in marriage, but are like angels in heaven" (Mark 12:25). This statement is a response to a question concerning family relationships in the afterlife. Such relationships are part of the order of terrestrial existence; they do not have bearing on any future existence. However, some theologians have argued that the church leader should proleptically display the quality of life of the age to come and should do this by refusing to marry. The problem with this reasoning is that abstaining from marriage produces only half a sign. Presumably the lack of necessity for marriage is the result of an existence in which the body is other than physical and relationships with people are of a quality different from that which is experienced by human beings in the present. So until those changes come about, it would seem to be anachronistic to reject the means of communication and relationship which God has ordained as appropriate to earthly existence.

The Pauline teaching on celibacy is also relevant here. Although neither Paul nor Barnabas were married, Paul indicates that in this respect he and Barnabas represented the exception rather than the rule. It is true that Paul does express the sentiment, "I wish that all were as I myself am," but he hastens to add that "each has his own special gift from God, one of one kind and one of another" (1 Cor. 7:7). Paul is addressing these remarks not to church leaders alone, but to all Christians. Marriage brings divided interests: "The unmarried man is anxious about the affairs of the Lord, how to please the Lord; but the married man is anxious about worldly affairs, how to please his wife, and his interests are divided" (1 Cor. 7:32-34). Paul speaks in an eschatological framework "in view of the impending distress" when he exhorts Christians to hold material goods and family relationships lightly (1 Cor. 7:26-31). But his general advice to the community as a whole is that "each man should have his own wife and each woman her own husband" (1 Cor. 7:2). And Paul states clearly that within marriage sexual intercourse is a wholesome activity to be enjoyed not only when procreation of children is anticipated, but regularly for mutual satisfaction. "Do not refuse one another except perhaps by agreement for a season . . . but then come together again" (1 Cor. 7:5). "Spiritual marriage," the practice of being together as husband and wife but not sharing the physical relationship of marriage, is not to be encouraged within the Christian community. Paul maintains that the single state is good and acceptable and is indeed a special gift as meaningful as that of marriage. The Christian who marries does well; the Christian who chooses not to marry also does well (1 Cor. 7:38). Either way it is a matter of choice. No special principles are stated for church leaders only. These instructions apply to all.

The Pastoral Epistles also address this issue. Timothy is reminded that he must select church leaders with great care. A bishop, for example, must be "above reproach." Candidates for this office should be married men. The measure of success they demonstrate in managing their family affairs is to be an important factor in considering their potential ability to handle a church leadership position. It stands to reason that "if a man does not know how to manage his own household, how can he care for God's church?" And the same applies to the office of deacon

(1 Tim. 3:1–7, 12). Timothy himself, however, does not appear to have been a married man at this time. He is a young man with strong passions which must be kept under control. Whether he later married is not known. The church situation reflected here is similar to that found in 1 Corinthians. The normal practice in the early church was to appoint married people to leadership positions, but there were exceptions. Single people, too, might hold positions of responsibility and hold them with honor.

Patristic Literature

Given this New Testament background, why is it that in the patristic period an ascetic ideal developed, in particular the celibacy of the priesthood? Many influences contributed to this development. First, the early church struggled for survival within a social and cultural milieu that was sexually promiscuous. Clement of Alexandria, writing in the third century C.E., deplored the fact that in rich households the proximity of male and female servants led to all kinds of abuse. Women in these households "bathe with their own servants, and strip naked before their slaves, and are rubbed by them." The public baths of the time were open to both male and female bathers: "There they strip for licentious indulgence (for from looking, men get to loving)" ("The Instructor," 3:5, in *ANF* 2:279). And in athletic contests male and female bodies were openly displayed. Such freedom inevitably led to unwelcome pregnancies, and as a result the practice of abortion flourished. In addition, unwanted infants were abandoned by their mothers and left to die.

Small wonder that the nascent church in reaction to such moral degradation cultivated the virtue of self-control and honored the celibate state. Clement of Alexandria himself chose to live a celibate life "out of love for the Lord." Clement expressed the opinion that God gives to some a special gift which makes a celibate life possible, and that those to whom this gift is given should be honored. But it is not to be assumed that celibacy is for all, nor that marriage is for all. "For every one is not to marry, nor always. But there is a time in which it is suitable, and a person for whom it is suitable" (The Stromata, 2:23, "On Marriage," in *ANF*, 2:377). Clement did, however, strongly emphasize the value of marriage. And of the two states, he was inclined to think marriage the most commendable. "One is not really shown to be a man in the choice of single life; but he surpasses men, who, disciplined by marriage, procreation of children, and care for the house . . . has been inseparable from God's love" (7:12, in *ANF*, 2:543). And in another place, Clement recalled that in some circles it was considered "unmanly and weak to shun living with a wife and children" (2:23, in *ANF*, 2:378).

A second influence which encouraged some within the church to idealize celibacy as a significant virtue involves a particular attitude toward human sexuality. In the Gnostic system of thought, God is considered to be immutable spiritual substance, but man, being estranged from God, finds himself encumbered with a physical body. This corporeal state is for him "a punishment and a purifying prison,"[4] and man must struggle to release himself from this. In some Gnostic circles it was felt that to indulge in the physical pleasures of sexual union would be to exploit the "fallen state," whereas to resist the passions would show that effort was being made to ascend toward spiritual union with God.

Although Gnosticism is diametrically opposed to Christianity, its influence was felt strongly in Christian circles. Origen, for example, a prolific Christian writer of the third century C.E., adopted an ascetic lifestyle.[5] Eusebius, in his *Ecclesiastical History* (Book 6), describes how Origen at an early age chose to "live like a philosopher . . . divesting himself of all the substance of youthful desires." For Origen, this involved fasting, limiting sleep, walking barefoot, enduring cold and nakedness, living in poverty, and abstaining from "the use of wine and all other things unnecessary for sustenance" (*FC*, 29:10-11). In his youthful ardor of devotion to the Christian ideal as he understood it, Origen went as far as to castrate himself, interpreting Matthew 19:12 ("there are eunuchs who have made themselves eunuchs for the sake of the kingdom of heaven") in a literal sense. Eusebius clearly disapproved of this and described it as "an act characteristic of an immature and youthful mind" (*FC*, 29:16). Origen's writings, however, show that although he regarded virginity as "the model of perfection," he did not require that church leaders be celibate. Assuming the Pastoral Epistles to be Pauline, and being convinced that the scriptural basis of church tradition was highly important, Origen affirmed the injunction that both male and female leaders in the church should be or have been married people. Origen did not approve of recommendations that married ecclesiastics should live separately from their wives. In his commentary on Matthew 5:32 he states that a man can cause his wife to commit adultery in ways other than by divorcing her. "He who withholds himself from his wife makes her oftentimes to be an adultress when he does not satisfy her desires, even though he does so under the appearance of greater gravity and self control" (*ANF*, 10:511). In the writings of Origen, the call to celibacy does not necessarily coincide with the call to ecclesiastical leadership.

A third factor which influenced the development of asceticism and celibacy was the rise of Montanism in the early centuries of the Christian Era. This movement originated in Phrygia under the leadership of Montanus during the second century C.E. and quickly spread to Italy, Africa, and Southern Gaul. Although strongly opposed by some leading churchmen, the movement flourished for several centuries, and traces of it can still be identified today. Montanus claimed that he was endued with a special effluence of the Paraclete such as had been promised by Jesus according to the Gospel of John (John 14:16). Under this direct guidance of the Holy Spirit, Montanus called into being a spiritual élite who were to restore the church to its original simplicity, making full use of charismatic gifts. He taught that the end of the world was imminent, and he attempted to gather "the chosen" into a community free from political and social relations with the state. He renamed

Pepuza, a small town in western Phrygia, Jerusalem, and it became the focus of the group's eschatological hopes.

Montanus shared leadership of the group with two prophetesses, Priscilla and Maximilla, who were greatly honored by the community and became the recipients of lavish gifts of money and clothing. They too participated in this unique possession of the Spirit, and their religious raptures led them to communicate spiritual truths which superseded those imparted by Christ, thus demonstrating that the age of revelation had not passed. Eusebius included the Montanists in his discussion of strange heresies which, "like poisonous reptiles, crawled over Asia and Phrygia" (*FC,* 19:311).

Because of their belief in the proximity of the Parousia, the imminence of wars and rebellions, and the approaching end of the world, the Montanists strongly discouraged marriage. The two prophetesses, in order to be fully consecrated to God, left their husbands and devoted themselves to spiritual ministry. Perhaps they hoped that others would follow their example. In the early stages of the movement, new marriages were prohibited; later the emphasis moved to insistence on one marriage only, although continence was still strongly advised, and husbands and wives were encouraged to live separately to make this more feasible. Virginity was held in high honor, and the single state was lauded in exaggerated terms.

Such widespread influence was bound to infiltrate the church. The influence of the Montanists can be seen clearly in the writings of Tertullian. A specialist in literature, philosophy, and law, Tertullian devoted himself also to the writing of religious treatises. Between 195 C.E. and 220 C.E. he wrote prolifically, and his works are acclaimed second only to those of Augustine (a fifth-century writer). So influential have these Latin writings been that some would describe Tertullian as the greatest writer of the patristic period. During his literary career, Tertullian was strongly influenced by Montanism, and around 212 C.E. he finally left the church and became the leader of a sect which bore his name, the

Tertullianists. Jerome claims that Tertullian was once a priest, but there is no reference to this in Tertullian's own writings, and Jerome's statement has been questioned. We are certain, however, that he was a married man, and two of his treatises provide us with insight into his changing convictions on the subject of marriage.

In the first treatise, *To His Wife*, Tertullian expresses a positive attitude toward marriage. "We do not read anywhere at all that marriage is forbidden; and this for the obvious reason that marriage is actually a good" (*ACW*, XIII, 12). He concludes the treatise with a sensitive eulogy on the married state:

> How beautiful, then, the marriage of two Christians, two who are one in hope, one in desire, one in the way of life they follow, one in the religion they practice. . . . They have no secrets from one another; they never shun each other's company; they never bring sorrow to each other's hearts. . . . Psalms and hymns they sing to one another. . . . Hearing and seeing this, Christ rejoices. To such as these He gives His peace. 'Where there are two together', there also He is present, and where He is, there evil is not (*ACW*, XIII, 35-36).

But Tertullian's second treatise, *An Exhortation to Chastity*, betrays the fact that Montanist ideas are beginning to permeate his thinking. Here he outlines three degrees of perfection, the highest of which is virginity from birth, or at least from baptism. The second degree involves "the mutual agreement of husband and wife to practice continence in marriage." The third degree is refusal to remarry after one's partner has died (*ACW*, XIII, 42). Marriage is "not so much a good as it is a kind of lesser evil" (*ACW*, XIII, 48) and one should make a distinction between "what God positively wills" and "what he merely allows."

In this second treatise Tertullian reflects on the Pauline teaching in 1 Corinthians 7:27-28 ("Are you free from a wife? Do not seek marriage. But if you marry, you do not sin"). He comes to the conclusion that permission to remarry after the death of one's spouse is only human counsel and is not a permission granted by God. He then introduces a rather weak argument: "We must acknowledge that a thing is forbidden by God when there is no evidence that He permits it" (*ACW*, XIII, 49). Tertullian justifies his negative assessment of marriage by drawing attention to the fact that God's original command to "increase and multiply" (Gen. 1:28) has now achieved its purpose. The world population has reached saturation point and therefore the Parousia must be near. For this reason Paul advised, "it remaineth that they also who have wives act as if they had none" (1 Cor. 7:29; *ACW*, XIII, 52). Marriage is not necessarily good because it is "lawful." It is only good if it is seen to be also "beneficial." Intercourse will lead to conception, and Tertullian speaks disparagingly of "swelling wombs and breasts and infants" (*ACW*, XIII, 58). "Children," he writes, "are a troublesome burden, especially in our times" (*ACW*, XIII, 61). "To think that Christians should be concerned about posterity—Christians for whom there is no tomorrow!" (*ACW*, XIII, 60-61).

Even though the Roman Catholic church does not accord Tertullian a place of honor among the fathers of the church, his writings have had a lasting impact on Christian thought. It is difficult for a lay person to distinguish between that material in Tertullian which represents something approximating to a Christian norm and that which has been colored by Montanist heresy. Consequently, many of his aberrant ideas and attitudes have permeated the Christian tradition through the centuries, and sadly some of these are still evident today.

There were two more influences which led Christians in the early centuries to idealize celibacy. One was the portrayal of women and family life in a somewhat negative light in the literature of the times, and the other was the rise of monasticism. Unfortunately, these two often went hand in hand. Some of the great leaders of the monastic movement showed a marked lack of respect for the married state and a strong tendency to depict virginity as superior to marriage. This attitude may be traced in the works of many of the patristic writers of the fourth and fifth centuries C.E., such as Gregory of Nyssa, John Chrysostom, Ambrose, and Augustine. But nowhere is it more forcibly expressed than in the writings of Jerome.

Jerome is best known for his work in Bible translation. He provided the church with a Latin translation of the Bible (popularly known as the Vulgate) which has substantially influenced English translations up to the present day. His early years were spent in Rome and his later years in Bethlehem where he organized and supervised monastic communities. Jerome's dedication to scholarly activity involved him in numerous controversies with other Christian thinkers. His correspondence with friends and his dogmatic treatises speak clearly on the issues of marriage and virginity.[6]

Although Jerome did not condemn family life, he evidently regarded it with disfavor. Marriage, he claims, was instituted by God at a time when it was necessary to "increase and multiply and replenish the earth" (Gen. 1:28). This good having been achieved, Jerome can see no justification for marriage except that it is a concession to those who lack self-control and that it holds within it the possibility of producing offspring who will be virgins. He focuses on the "troubles" which accompany family life—"the crying of infants, the death of children, the chance of abortion" (*NPNF,* 6:77), and on the "drawbacks" of marriage—"pregnancy . . . the torture caused by a rival, the cares of household management, and all those fancied blessings which death at last cuts short" (*NPNF,* 6:23).

Virginity, Jerome maintains, compares with marriage as gold with silver. It is "cleaner than wedlock," and "all who have not remained virgins are reckoned as defiled" (*NPNF,* 6:78, 74). Reading that Paul permits married couples to abstain from sexual intercourse by mutual agreement for periods of prayer (1 Cor. 7:5), Jerome draws the unwarranted conclusion that prayer is only possible when a person abstains from sexual intercourse, and if one is to maintain a constant attitude of prayer, then the state of virginity is essential (*NPNF,* 6:75). Mary is extolled as the model of virginity, and Jerome violently attacks the opinion of Helvidius, one of his contemporaries, who claimed on the basis of Matthew 12:46 and Luke 8:20 that after the birth of Jesus, Mary and Joseph enjoyed normal marital relations. Even Joseph, Jerome argues, remained perpetually virgin "so that a virgin son might be born of a virgin wedlock" (*FC*, 53:39). Thus for Jerome the holy family has paradoxically become a model of virginity!

Married Christians are exhorted to aim toward a life of abstinence from sexual intercourse, particularly after they have borne children. "Let them begin with short periods of release from the marriage bond, and give themselves unto prayer, that when they have tasted the sweets of chastity they may desire the perpetual possession of that wherewith they were temporarily delighted" (*NPNF*, 6:355). "If you only have patience," Jerome exhorts, "your wife will some day become your sister" (*NPNF*, 6:69). This applies particularly to married people in church leadership positions. "Those persons who are chosen to be bishops, priests and deacons are either virgins or widowers; or at least when once they have received the priesthood, are vowed to perpetual chastity" (*NPNF*, 6:79). "You will surely admit that he is no bishop who during his episcopate begets children" (*NPNF*, 6:371). A married man who becomes a priest "must always be released from the duties of marriage" (*NPNF*, 6:372).

Although Jerome was aware that there were many lapses from this standard, it did not occur to him that it might be the nature of the rule which was inappropriate. He simply condemned the hypocritical attitudes of those who professed one lifestyle but practiced another. He does admit, however, that he himself is not without censure in these matters. "I extol virginity to the skies, not because I myself possess it, but because, not possessing it, I admire it all the more. . . . The weight of my body keeps me fixed to the ground" (*NPNF*, 6:78). Jerome hints at the sensuous longings which sometimes overtook him amidst the privations of his desert sojourns and gives the reader insight concerning his early years in Rome. "How often did I fancy myself among the pleasures of

Rome! . . . I often found myself amid bevies of girls" (*NPNF*, 6:25). Indeed, when Jerome finally left Rome for Bethlehem it was under a dark cloud of scandal concerning his relationships with some Roman women whom he was purportedly encouraging in a life of self-denial. One of the women, a wealthy widow named Paula, followed him to Bethlehem and worked with him there, founding ascetical communities for women. The deep feelings Jerome entertained for Paula are clearly evidenced in his letters.

Some of Jerome's fellow churchmen had reservations about opinions such as these. Nevertheless, the ascetic ideal which he proposed with such vigor held an attraction and profoundly influenced the life of the church from that time onward. Within the Christian communities, family life was downgraded and sexual intercourse was regarded as something unclean. At best it could only have a utilitarian purpose—the procreation of children. The "perfect" Christian was one who denied himself or herself the fulfillment of sensual desires and particularly sexual desires. As the monastic communities spread through the Mediterranean world, it became customary to appoint church leaders from this group of people. They comprised the literate minority at a time when education was denied to the masses. Gradually their lifestyle, rather than being regarded as one particular vocation for a Christian to pursue, came to be viewed as the ideal lifestyle of a Christian. It was therefore considered to be the only acceptable lifestyle for one who was to be appointed to a leadership position within the church.

Church Councils

The impact of these various influences which exalted celibacy within the early Christian communities was felt at the councils held during this period. The Council of Elvira, which met c. 300 C.E. and which hosted representatives of thirty-seven communities (mainly from southern Spain where the council was held), adopted a number of canons in an effort to bring about reforms in a church which was fast deteriorating under the influence of pagan customs.

One of these was the famous *Canon 33,* which is the earliest known written law dealing with the matter of celibacy.

> We decree that all bishops, priests, deacons, and all clerics engaged in the ministry are forbidden entirely to live with their wives and to beget children: whoever shall do so will be deprived from the clerical dignity.[7]

This is an indication that many clergy of the time were married. But it also demonstrates that what had once been a matter of choice was now becoming a matter of law. The implication of the canon was that church leadership and marital relations were incompatible, and this implication was to lend strong support to the belief that the ideal church leader was actually a celibate person. There was, as a result, a growing tendency to select church leaders from the ranks of those who had chosen a celibate lifestyle.

The matter was raised again at the first general council of the church, which was convened by Emperor Constantine (325 C.E.). This council was comprised of about three hundred bishops, although almost all of them were from the eastern half of the empire. The council met at Nicea (modern Iznik, northeast Turkey). The Spanish bishop, Hosius of Cordoba, was present as Constantine's adviser. A strong effort was made to introduce for acceptance on this wider level many of the canons of the Council of Elvira. Fourteen of the Spanish canons were accepted, but some were not. *Canon 33* in particular was rejected. It was argued that the intercourse of a man with his wife is chaste intercourse and should not be forbidden. To forbid it would not only put an unreasonable demand on the man, but would also threaten the virtue of his wife. "Marriage and married intercourse are of themselves honorable and undefiled" (*NPNF,* 14:51).

The Council of Gangra, a local council meeting near Ankara, Turkey, some time prior to 341 C.E., was also concerned about the excessive emphasis the church was placing on asceticism. An extremist, Eustathius of Sebaste, was teaching that celibacy was the ideal way of life for all Christians and was indeed necessary for salvation. The council introduced some twenty canons in opposition to this and also denounced those church members who were refusing to attend worship celebrated by married priests.

Gradually there came about a difference between the Latin church and the Greek church in relation to this issue. The Latin church began to insist that bishops, priests, deacons, and subdeacons should not marry after taking holy orders. If they had married prior to this, they must live separate from their wives. The Greek church permitted the local bishop to decide whether a deacon or subdeacon might marry after ordination. Clergy in the Greek church were forbidden to leave their wives under the pretext of piety, but after the death of a wife, no second marriage was permitted. By degrees the Greek church encouraged its bishops and higher clergy to live in celibacy, though the letter of Synesius (early fifth century C.E.) shows that the personal decision of the candidate was respected. Synesius declared that he would refuse consecration if it meant leaving his wife and forgoing the possibility of raising children. He was appointed Bishop of Ptolemais nevertheless.

It was not until the time of the Reformation in the sixteenth century C.E. that a serious challenge was again issued to the concept of a celibate clergy. At this time Martin Luther, a German priest, led a movement to bring about much-needed reforms in many aspects of the church's life. In particular he voiced the opinion that much of the teaching of the early fathers had obscured the meaning of the Christian faith and in some cases had actually distorted it. For example, Luther argued, the emphasis the early fathers had placed on asceticism and celibacy had led to a depreciation of the value placed on marriage. Luther condemned the leaders of the church for insisting that a married man could not fulfill the priestly office.

> That is as much as to say that marriage is harlotry, sin, impure, and rejected by God. And even though they say at the same time, that marriage is holy and a sacrament, that is hypocrisy and a lie, for if they would sincerely regard it as holy and a sacrament, they would not forbid a priest to marry.[8]

Luther called on church people to reexamine the teachings of the Bible and to live their lives in accordance with the principles found there. As a result, many of the clergy married and raised families. Luther himself married Katherina von Bora, who since the age of five had been raised first in a Benedictine order and then in a Cistercian order. Together they raised six children of their own and eleven orphans, living frugally on a small stipend as Luther refused to accept extra monies offered to him for his teaching. In this way he combined the true monastic spirit with a meaningful dedication to family life.

The Roman Catholic church reacted to the Reformation teaching by calling a council which over a period of eighteen years (1545–1563) met in twenty-five sessions to bring about reforms of its own within the church structure. The decrees of the Council of Trent (Italy) insisted that traditions handed down through the church from age to age were to be treated with as much reverence as canonical Scripture. The Lutheran position on marriage and celibacy was opposed. It was reaffirmed that marriage and priesthood were incompatible and that celibacy was to be a condition required of those entering holy orders. In these matters the Roman Catholic church has differed in practice from the Reformation churches up to the present day.

Twentieth-Century Attitudes

Orthodox

Current practices in Orthodox churches regarding a married or celibate clergy stem from diverse traditions. In the fourth and fifth centuries C.E. there were many married bishops who lived with their wives as "brother and sister." In the sixth century C.E. it was decreed that married men might still be appointed bishops, but only if they were childless. The ostensible reason was that without the responsibilities of fatherhood the bishop would be freer to devote himself to spiritual matters. Another consideration, however, was the inheritance of church property. Children of deceased clergy might claim as their rightful inheritance monies which would otherwise accrue to the church. Many churches, therefore, preferred to appoint unmarried bishops, or at least childless bishops.

The official position of the Orthodox churches concerning celibacy was formulated during the Second Trullan Synod, 692 C.E. A distinction was made between the appointment of a bishop and the appointment of a priest, deacon, or subdeacon. A bishop must be a person who lived in continence. If a married man was appointed as bishop, the marriage was to be ended by mutual consent, the wife being encouraged to enter a monastery far removed geographically from her husband's bishopric. At the present time, however, there are Orthodox communities which appoint married men as bishops and permit them to live normal family lives. Married bishops are found, for example, in the Nestorian church, in the Ukrainian Orthodox Autocephalous church, and among the Monophysites of Egypt and Ethiopia.

Priests, deacons, and subdeacons were to be appointed freely from the ranks of married men and were not to separate from their wives. The Eastern church strongly resisted pressure from the Latin church to change this practice. To require these men to live in celibacy was to require more than Jesus himself had required. Orthodox clerics were exhorted to continence only on days contiguous to those of divine service. If the wife died, however, the cleric was expected not to remarry. If he did, the children of the second union were considered illegitimate. This ruling is treated with reserve by the orthodox churches today. Widowed clerics may assume a lower office in the church and thus be freed to remarry. Marriage is prohibited only to men who are ordained to clerical status while still single.[9]

Roman Catholic

The Roman Catholic position on celibacy has altered very little with the passage of time. According to canon law, only celibate men may be appointed to the higher orders. The reasons adduced for this are that "the state of virginity is in itself more perfect, a celibate clergy is more effective, enjoys greater respect and authority, and follows the example of Christ and the Apostles, and the teaching of the Fathers of the Church."[10] Those who choose to mary after ordination fall *ipso jure* from the clerical state. In 1920, Pope Benedict XV declared: "We solemnly testify that the Holy See will never in any way mitigate, much less abolish, this most sacred and salutary law."[11]

In 1965, this stance was confirmed by the decrees of Vatican II. "The Ministry and Life of Priests" states the position thus:

> Celibacy, which at first was recommended to priests, was afterwards in the Latin Church imposed by law on all who were to be promoted to holy Orders. This sacred Council approves and confirms this legislation so far as it concerns those destined for the priesthood.[12]

Pope Paul VI stated that it was his intention "to give new luster and strength to priestly celibacy in the world of today." Although many were questioning the bond which linked celibacy and priesthood, Paul VI stated that "the present law of celibacy should today continue to be firmly linked to the ecclesiastical ministry."[13]

More than ten years later, in his "Letter to all Priests," Pope John Paul II reflected on the fact that objections to this stance had intensified during the post-conciliar period. He denied the view that celibacy is "imposed by law on those who receive the sacrament of Orders." Rather, he maintained, "Every Christian who receives the sacrament of Orders commits himself to celibacy with full awareness and freedom."[14] Nevertheless, the fact remains that unless a person does so commit himself to celibacy, he may not be ordained as a priest. And if, as a priest, he chooses to marry, he is deprived of his clerical status. Today the issue is still causing considerable unease in the Roman Catholic church. A recent ruling does permit deacons to be married, but they may not then use the diaconate as a step to the priesthood. Only celibate deacons may become priests.

The Roman Catholic church is not altogether consistent with respect to celibacy. It does, for example, permit married clergy to continue to officiate in the Eastern churches. These Uniate churches are Orthodox churches which have aligned themselves with the Roman Catholic tradition. Vatican II states:

> While recommending ecclesiastical celibacy this sacred Council does not by any means aim at changing that contrary discipline which is lawfully practiced in the Eastern Churches. Rather the Council affectionately exhorts all those who have received the priesthood in the married state to persevere in their holy vocation and continue to devote their lives fully and generously to the flock entrusted to them.[15]

Recently, however, when Pope John Paul II used a March, 1980, Synod of Ukrainian Catholic bishops to bring this Eastern rite church under the control of Rome, it was made clear that the Ukranians would not be permitted to continue the practice of ordaining married men as priests. So the issue has by no means been laid to rest.

Protestant

Generally speaking, in Protestant churches today there is no particular written requirement concerning the marital status of a church leader, except in respect to divorce. In practice, however, most Protestant churches prefer leaders to be married. The reasons for this are sometimes stated but more often implied. A single young man may be regarded with suspicion because the aura of holiness which surrounds his appointment may make him attractive to young women in the congregation, and the opportunities afforded him in counseling and visiting may become a source of temptation leading to immoral relationships. Churches which fear the development of such a situation have often refused to appoint a single person to ministry, advising him to "find a wife" first and then come back to apply for a position.

Unhappily, this means that a male applicant who has chosen a single lifestyle and who would prefer to remain single often finds difficulty in obtaining a church leadership position. His sexual identity may be questioned and his relationships with younger men in the congregation may be carefully observed. Cultural norms and the attitudes of secular society apparently carry more weight than scriptural teaching. It is rare in Protestant circles to find an affirmation of the biblical perspective on celibacy. Few Protestant congregations accord honor to those who embrace a celibate lifestyle, and the comparative absence of celibate clergy in these churches is a symptom of such an attitude.

In practical terms, a church which appoints a married minister is gaining far more than a healthy role model of Christian family life. It is gaining a spouse who, although not included on the payroll of the church, is expected to be committed to the church's life and ministry. Traditionally this unpaid worker has been the wife. Frequently she is actively involved in Christian education, church music, and supervision of janitorial duties, flower arrangements, and banquets. She may also assist in counseling and in practical support as specific needs arise within the church community. In addition, she is expected to provide hospitality to a wide cross section of the church's membership. Small wonder that Protestant churches have shown such a marked preference for married ministers.

As more churches are now appointing women as ministers, it will be interesting to see whether this trend continues. Will it be assumed that there should be alongside the woman minister a husband who can move into the congregation as an unpaid worker? The way our society is structured, it is unlikely that a husband would be free to participate to such an extent. As churches realize this, will they perhaps prefer to appoint, ironically, a celibate woman rather than a married woman to the leadership position? A celibate woman, after all, could give undivided loyalty to the congregation and, being free from family responsibilities, would be able to contribute more hours of service to the church community!

If such reasoning does triumph, it will provide a powerful example of how much stronger are cultural pressures than the scriptural principles Protestants so enthusiastically avow.

Conclusions

In a previous chapter it was noted that the concept of the church leader as a priest led to an association of ideas which excluded women from holding such an office. The development of the concept of a celibate priesthood removed women one stage further from effective influence in the leadership of the church. Attempts to ensure that the celibate priest preserved a standard of moral purity led to an atmosphere in which he was discouraged from developing any meaningful relationships with women. In his social life he was encouraged to restrict himself to male company or to associate only with women who were much older than himself. The women who cared for his house were servants, not partners. The church leader was thus estranged from the influence of women in his personal as well as his professional life. And yet he was to exercise a leadership role in a community which was at least 50 percent women and to make decisions which profoundly affected their lives. Over the centuries the church has thus created a polarity of the sexes, and this problem must now be addressed. Some Protestant churches have overreacted by insisting that the church leader must be a married person. In so doing, these churches overlook the very positive contribution which can be made by a celibate leader.

The church of today must distinguish between the call to celibacy and the call to ministry. The call to celibacy is a personal issue which only the individual concerned can rightly assess. The call to church leadership is a matter of community decision. In making that decision, the community should bear in mind the fact that there is room for great diversity in leadership roles.

Of course, there are many areas in which it would not make any difference whether the church leader was married or single.

Neither marriage nor celibacy alone provides the individual with the qualities needed for church leadership. Neither state protects the individual from sexual temptation, or ensures moral purity. The church must be open to the possibility that effective leadership can be provided by either the married or the celibate individual. Ideally, all churches—Protestant, Orthodox, and Roman Catholic—should demonstrate this diversity when appointing men and women to leadership roles. In so doing, they would be aligning themselves with scriptural teaching and with the situation which existed in the early centuries of the Common Era, before alien influences caused some Chrsitian communities to adopt a low concept of marriage and family life.

Notes

[1] *Vatican Council II,* ed. A. Flannery (New York: Costello, 1975), p. 439.

[2] For a discussion of the origins of these sexual taboos in ancient civilizations, see R. R. Ruether, *Liberation Theology* (New York: Paulist, 1972), pp. 95-114.

[3] Jewish people still hold marriage in very high esteem and regard celibacy with misgivings. "Scripture represents marriage not merely as a Mosaic ordinance, but as part of the scheme of Creation, intended for all humanity." "Only through married life does human personality reach its highest fulfillment." "The celibate life is the unblessed life: Judaism requires its saints to show their saintliness IN the world, and amid the ties and obligations of family life." Joseph H. Hertz, *The Authorised Daily Prayer Book* (New York: Bloch Publishing Company, 1974), pp. 1006-1007.

[4] H. von Campenhausen, *The Fathers of the Greek Church,* trans. S. Godman (New York: Pantheon, 1959).

[5] The ascetic flavor of Stoic philosophy might also have influenced Origen's lifestyle.

[6] See J. N. D. Kelly, *Jerome* (New York: Harper & Row, 1975).

[7] Mansi 2.11 as quoted in *New Catholic Encyclopedia* 3:371.

[8] "On the Councils and the Church," *Luther's Works,* trans. Charles M. Jacobs (Philadelphia: Fortress, 1966), 41:163.

[9] See Petro B. T. Bilaniuk, "Celibacy and Eastern Tradition," *Celibacy: The Necessary Option,* ed. George H. Frein (New York: Herder & Herder, 1968), pp. 32-72.

[10] T. L. Bouscaren, A. C. Ellis, and F. N. Korth, *Canon Law: A Text and Commentary* (Milwaukee: Bruce, 1963), p. 544.

[11] Allocution 16, December 1920; *Acta Apostolicae Sedis* 12-585; Digest I:121, as quoted in Bouscaren, Ellis, and Korth, *Canon Law,* p. 114.

[12] *Vatican Council II,* p. 893.

[13]"The Celibacy of the Priest" *(Sacerdotalis Caelibatus),* Encyclical of Pope Paul VI (Huntington, Ind.: Our Sunday Visitor, 1968).

[14]*L'Osservatore Romano* N 16 (577), April 17, 1979.

[15]*Vatican Council II,* p. 892.

THE ORDINATION
OF WOMEN:
PRESENT-DAY ATTITUDES

NEARLY TWO THOUSAND years have passed since the first Christian communities came into being in the Eastern Mediterranean world. During these years the church has grown and developed and has fashioned for itself multifarious structures through which to channel its activities. Leadership models have been established, and for many church communities these have been exclusively male. During the present century, however, significant changes have been taking place. People have become more aware of oppression and discrimination in all its forms, and particularly as it relates to women. The impact of such attitudes is felt within the church, where women have for many years been deprived of honor and recognition in leadership positions. It is now widely recognized that there are scriptural and historical reasons for challenging customs which have led to male dominance in church leadership, and efforts are being made to examine these and to establish a church structure which gives equal honor to both sexes.

Generally speaking, Protestant churches have moved with greater rapidity in examining issues and in implementing new policies, but there are people within the Orthodox and Roman Catholic communities who are equally sensitive to the problems and whose views are being expressed. This chapter reviews some of the issues relating to women which are being debated in Christian communities today and indicates areas in which changes have come about.

The Orthodox Churches

In September, 1976, a consultation was held in Agapia, Roumania, on the role and participation of women in the Orthodox churches. Speakers from many different countries addressed the issue with perceptive insight. The keynote address was delivered by Elizabeth Behr-Sigel of France, who raised for consideration a number of questions dealing with significant topics.

Behr-Sigel notes with regret that pronouncements concerning women in the Orthodox churches have in the past been made by men, with little effort made to ascertain the opinions of the women whom they concern. Orthodox women, she maintains, are not necessarily happy about the place "assigned to them from time immemorial by nature and by Tradition."[1] Indeed, she claims, social customs and convention, rather than true theological insight, frequently govern attitudes toward women. Unhappily, women have been subordinated by social and cultural mechanisms; they have been separated from men and relegated to an inferior position. Somewhere along the line the church has overlooked the fact that "the revelation of the One God in three Persons . . . is reflected as the Creator's will in the multiplicity of persons and the unity of human nature in humanity."[2]

The patristic writers, Behr-Sigel states, made a significant contribution in changing the concept of women. They exalted consecrated virginity and thus showed an awareness of women's worth beyond mere biological function. Nevertheless, the patristic writings did not encourage a healthy reciprocal relationship between male and female members of the church.

It is for a healthy relationship that the church of today must strive. The women's liberation movement has tended toward the development of negative qualities—selfishness and a desire for power and domination—the very qualities which on the part of men have contributed to the present sad state of relationships within the church. "We do not experience the church as a pyramid of authority," Behr-Sigel comments. "We experience it . . . as a community of prayer and love."[3] What is needed is "an imaginative new style of relationships and new structures in which liberated men and women can join together . . . respecting one another's dignity and distinctiveness."[4]

Latent in the Orthodox churches' consciousness has always been the recognition that men and women are equal before God. But layers of prejudice and cultural conditioning have obscured this reality. Orthodox theologians have dismissed Galatians 3:26–28 as having reference to baptism rather than to the matter of ordination to priesthood. Behr-Sigel argues that "the fundamental ontological unity . . . created by baptism is the foundation of the royal priesthood of all the baptized in which the ministry has its origins as a special, personal vocation."[5] If women are to be denied the charism of priesthood, Behr-Sigel asks, "are we not in fact subordinating grace to a biological determinism?"[6]

With these penetrating observations and questions, Behr-Sigel leaves open the issue of the ordination of women to the priesthood in the Orthodox community. For her, the biggest problem concerning the ordination of women to a sacramental priesthood is that the bishop or priest is for the local congregation "the icon of the Word incarnate."[7] There is a mysterious correspondence between "the masculine and the Word" and "the feminine and the Spirit," and this must continue to be a topic of reflection and study.

The Agapia consultation has provided an effective starting point for such reflection, claiming that Orthodox women should have access to theological education and should be given the opportunity of teaching theology in Orthodox seminaries. A deaconess college has been founded in Greece, and the Coptic church in Egypt is consecrating women as deaconesses. Some Orthodox seminaries in the United States will admit women. Such trends are not novel. Up to the tenth century C.E. women served actively as deaconesses in the Orthodox churches, and Emperor Justinian lists as members of the clergy women who had received a major order. Hopefully the debate on these issues will continue until such attitudes become more pervasive.

The Roman Catholic Church

In the same year in which the Orthodox consultation was held in Agapia, Paul VI approved a statement on this subject entitled, "Declaration on the question of the admission of women to the ministerial priesthood."[8] This statement was intended to be representative of opinions held within the Roman Catholic church. Many Roman Catholic scholars, however, found the Declaration to be inadequate in its argumentation, and other more carefully researched material has since been published.

The Declaration signed by Paul VI avows that the ruling in *Gaudium et Spes* (7 December 1965) still holds true. That ruling stated that the Roman Catholic church is opposed to all discrimination, in particular that based on sex.[9] However, it is the church's tradition that women are to be excluded from the priesthood, and this tradition is to be adhered to at the present time. The Declaration recognizes that the patristic authors strongly influenced the policy of excluding women from leadership in the Roman Catholic church. It acknowledges that these writers are not beyond reproach. In the writings of the Fathers, "one will find the undeniable influence of prejudices unfavourable to women";[10] and medieval scholastic doctors "often present arguments . . . that modern thought would have difficulty in admitting or would even rightly reject."[11] However, the statement affirms that, "Since that period and up to our own time . . . the practice has enjoyed peaceful and universal acceptance."[12]

The Declaration states that in this as in all other matters it is the magisterium of the church which determines "what can change and what must remain immutable."[13] Unhappily this magisterium is almost exclusively male. It is claimed that the concept of an all-male priesthood is an unbroken tradition in both the East and the West—a claim that would be difficult to substantiate. While recognizing that some Roman Catholic women feel drawn to priestly vocations, the writers indicate that such "calling," while noble and understandable, is not genuine. It is purely subjective and is based on personal attraction. For a "call" to be genuine, it must be authenticated by the church.

The main theological argument used in this document against the ordination of women to the priesthood concerns the role of the priest in the eucharistic celebration. The priest it is claimed, acts *in persona Christi,* "taking the role of Christ to the point of being his very image." The value of a sign rests in the fact that it is perceptible, easily recognizable. It is claimed that "there would not be this 'natural resemblance' . . . if the role of Christ were not taken by a man."[14] It is acknowledged that at the eucharist the priest also represents the church (the bride of Christ), but this is considered secondary.

The Declaration of 1976 is all the more interesting because it was promulgated within a year of the Detroit Ordination Conference. This conference, held in November, 1975, was attended by 1400 men and women who were concerned to explore the matter of the ordination of women in the Roman Catholic church. Discussion at this conference ranged over a number of significant issues.[15]

Elizabeth Carroll reminded delegates that women are excluded not from service in the church but from official installation. Although called to priesthood, women are not satisfied with the concept of priesthood embraced by the Roman Catholic community. The formulative period for this particular office was the last half of the third century C.E. At that time antifeminism was deeply ingrained in Jewish and Greek tradition. It triumphed over the teachings of Jesus and Paul. What passes today as "sacred tradition" is in fact "not of divine origin, but only the prolongation of an inadequate response imposed on the gospel message by the dominant culture."[16]

Rosemary Reuther attributed the exclusion of women from church leadership not to "the order of creation," but to "the fallen disorder of injustice." She challenged the entire symbolism sustaining the Roman Catholic church's hierarchical structure—symbolism which speaks of power, lordship, and authority. Male dominance in the church is one of those injustices that must be overcome. Reuther lamented the fact that the persons who hold the power for change are elderly, Italian, male celibates, "persons whose entire personal, social and cultural experience most totally removes them from understanding the issues of women."[17] A new concept of teaching authority is needed, Reuther maintains, one which allows for fallibility and incompleteness in what the church has taught to past generations.

Anne Elizabeth Carr also challenged the present concept of leadership in the Roman Catholic church. Neither pope nor bishop nor priest, she claimed, can be found in the New Testament in the form in which these offices exist in the Roman Catholic church. No absolute forms of ministry were imposed by Jesus or the apostles. The exalting of the Mass and the diminishing of the centrality of the preaching of the Word came about as the result of choices made by various church officials.[18]

Richard McBrien commented on the fact that the Vatican II Council, while condemning the worldwide discrimination based on sex, did not face the problem within its own borders.[19] It is well-known that the conveners of the council even refused to allow a woman to read a paper before the assembly.[20]

Eleanor Kahle emphasized the practical problems involved in the ordination of women. She claimed that male priests were more threatened by the possibility of a change in the "lifestyle" of the rectory than they were by the concept of a woman celebrating Mass.[21]

Joseph Komonchak challenged the tenacity of tradition and the wisdom of accepting its dictates without question. Tradition must be understood, judged, and evaluated. He quoted Cyprian as saying that "a custom without truth is simply the antiquity of error." One must therefore consider carefully the issue of the ordination of women. If the reasons advanced against ordaining women are not valid, what authority does the mere custom have? And, Komonchak asked, what makes one tradition more sacred than another?[22]

The Roman Catholic church still prohibits the ordination of women to the priesthood. John Paul II has indicated that he does not intend to make any change in this situation. In 1979, however, the *Catholic Biblical Quarterly* published a summary of the findings of a task force appointed in 1976 to study the topic, "Women and Priestly Ministry: The New Testament Evidence."[23] The task force consisted of prominent scholars selected from the ranks of the Catholic Biblical Association of America.

These scholars remarked that the New Testament does not provide materials dealing specifically with the role of women in the ministry of Jesus or in the conduct of early church life. The material for consideration in the New Testament is sporadic and geared to particular situations. Moreover, the Christian priesthood as embodied in the structure of the Roman Catholic church came into being after the period of the New Testament documents. The concept of ministry reflected in the New Testament is that of diverse charisms distributed widely among various members of the community. No one group controlled or exercised all of the ministries. The task force pointed out that the coming of the kingdom of God transformed the old social order. Women featured prominently among the disciples of Jesus from the beginning of his ministry until the end, becoming in fact the first witnesses of the resurrection. Women thus met the Pauline criterion for apostleship. Women were present within the Christian community at Pentecost and shared in the outpouring of the Spirit, from which derived the gifts which equipped for ministry. Women ministered along with men in founding churches, leading public worship, and teaching new converts. Such roles were ultimately associated with priestly ministry, and they were evidently never restricted to men.

One argument frequently used by those who oppose the ordination of women is that Jesus chose twelve men to be his apostles. He selected no women for this honor. Consequently women should not be ordained as priests. The task force challenged the validity of this line of reasoning. Not only were there no women among the Twelve—there were no Gentiles, no Samaritans, and no slaves as far as can be ascertained. Did Jesus intend to establish a criterion for office with respect to race, ethnic identity, and social status? If not, why would his choice delineate a criterion for office with respect to sex? In addition, it is clear from the pages of the New Testament that at no time were the roles and functions now associated with the priestly ministry restricted to the Twelve. Indeed, apostolic ministry itself was shared by a wider group of people, some of whom are named in the New Testament. But apostleship was not an office which could be handed on by succession. It was in a sense an eschatological role which passed with time. And the basic task of ministry was always shared among a much wider group—people who were prophets, teachers, administrators, and so on—a group that was never exclusively male. It is this group from which the priestly ministry stems.

The task force expressed the opinion that "the claim that the intention and example of Jesus and the example of the apostles provide a norm excluding women from priestly ministry cannot be sustained on either logical or historical grounds."[24] The only prohibitions against women participating in worship are pastoral directives motivated by social and cultural factors. Such texts cannot be used to support the exclusion of women from church office. "The conclusion we drew, then, is that the New Testament evidence, while not decisive by itself, points towards the admission of women to priestly ministry."[25]

Moving even more directly into the matter of women ordained to the priesthood is a study conducted by Fran Ferder entitled, *Called to Break Bread?*[26] Ferder notes that the documents emanating from Vatican II inspired women to assume more commitment to the life of the church and to its task in the world. Placed before them was a new vision of equality, and women were urged to increase their knowledge of Scripture and to develop their inner potential so that they might follow the vocational destiny assigned to them by God. As women responded to this challenge, many felt called to priestly ministry. This was interpreted by some church officials not as a vocation to be joyfully affirmed, but as a threat to the church which must be countered. "It appeared," Ferder writes, "that the vision and ideal of the Second Vatican Council had gone beyond the cultural and emotional limitations of the church at this moment of history."[27]

The study conducted by Ferder addressed itself to three basic questions: Who are the women who wish to test a call to ordination in the Catholic church? What are they like as women and as ministers? Why do they want to be priests? The study involved one hundred women who felt so called. The majority of them were physically attractive, highly educated, intelligent women in whose lives Scripture reading and daily prayer featured prominently. They proved to be people with confidence and a basic sense of personal security. They were thoughtful and articulate people, open minded and well-balanced in social attitudes, and they related well in individual and group situations. It became clear to the interviewers that these people were not seeking ordination to the priesthood because of any excessive desire for power or status. Nor were they strong supporters of the women's liberation movement. They were women with an inner awareness that God had equipped them with gifts for priestly office and that God was calling them to bring these gifts to fruition in the service of the church.

The Roman Catholic community in the United States is becoming increasingly aware of the need to ordain women to the sacramental priesthood. Time will tell how closely the governmental mechanisms of the church are geared to the mind of its peoples.

The Protestant Churches

Within some Protestant denominations the ordination of women to ministry is so well-established that it no longer calls for comment. Sometimes, however, a wide gap remains between theory and practice. The following paragraphs communicate some of the issues with which Protestant denominations are still grappling. This is not a comprehensive survey. Unfortunately, time and resources precluded such. Rather, it is a sampling of the present situation in some of the leading denominations in the United States of America. It is important to note, however, that there is lively discussion of this issue in some of the smaller evangelical denominations, and that attitudes and policies are gradually changing in the Conservative Baptist Association, the General Association of Regular Baptists, the Grace Brethren Church, the Plymouth Brethren, the Free Methodist Church, the Evangelical Free Church, the Reformed Presbyterian Church, and other such groups. A more wide-ranging survey would be most valuable.

Assemblies of God, General Council

Many Pentecostal churches have always assumed that as the Holy Spirit is given by God irrespective of the sex of the recipient, so the ministries conferred by the Spirit are to be exercised irrespective of the sex of the recipient. This principle, however, is not always clearly reflected in the statistics of church structure. The General Council of the Assemblies of God, for example, has in its present bylaws a statement concerning the ordination of women which is practically identical to that embodied in the first constitution of the church (1914). The current statement reads as follows:

> *Eligibility of women.* The Scriptures plainly teach that divinely called and qualified women may also serve the church in the Word (Joel 2:28; Acts 21:9; 1 Corinthians 11:5). Women who have developed in the ministry of the Word so that their ministry is acceptable generally, and who have proved their qualifications in actual service, and who have met all the requirements of

the credentials committees of the district councils, are entitled to whatever grade of credentials their qualifications warrant and the right to administer the ordinances of the church when such acts are necessary.[28]

By late 1977, this denomination was listing nearly 1600 ordained women, with another 1600 women licensed to perform ministerial duties. However, only 292 women are pastors of churches. This means that only 3 percent of the 9,214 churches in the denomination have women pastors. Many of these are small churches which would have difficulty obtaining a male pastor. Of the other women with ministerial credentials, 95 are listed as "home missionaries," 309 as "foreign missionaries," 1,225 are "retired," and 1,256 are "pastor's wives, evangelists, teachers, inactive, etc." The ordained women who are pastor's wives share in the ministry of their husbands and may or may not carry the title of "pastor."

Joseph R. Flower, the general secretary of this denomination, has produced an unofficial statement entitled, "Does God deny spiritual manifestations and ministry gifts to women?" This paper, written in 1978, is a historical and exegetical study exposing some of the misconceptions and prejudices which in the past have prevented people from accepting women in the role of minister. Flower notes that the influence of Christ did much to restore the dignity of women in a world which had relegated them to a position of social inferiority. Flower maintains that theologically speaking, the death of Christ released humanity from the curse brought about by sin. Woman is no longer to be subjugated under male headship. The mutual and complementary relationship that Adam and Eve enjoyed before the fall may now be restored, and the church should be in the vanguard of any movement which aims to restore this balance in a scriptural framework.

The American Baptist Convention

The American Baptist Convention officially endorsed the idea of ordained women serving as pastors in the late nineteenth century. Names of the earliest women ministers have not survived, although it is known that the second woman to be ordained by this denomination was ordained in Nebraska in the 1890s. However, at this present time, of the 6,609 ordained ministers in American Baptist churches, only 248 are women. This low percentage is a cause for concern to some members of the denomination. A survey entitled "A Study of Women in Ministry," which was conducted over a two-year period, 1976–1978, confirmed suspicions that women are discriminated against in seminaries, among executive and area ministers, among pulpit committee representatives, and among the laity. The survey indicated that women are at a disadvantage in the recruitment/placement system, that it is more difficult for women to find an appointment than it is for men, and that women receive lower salary and allowances than their male counterparts.[29]

Why this difference between theory and practice? The answer is found in the fact that each local church is autonomous. The individual congregation may choose to appoint or to refuse a woman as minister. Members of a congregation naturally tend to be influenced by cultural forces and by custom. Some congregations have not been educated to move beyond the "traditional" when considering the role of women. Thus, appointing a woman as minister becomes a point of controversy. Pulpit committees will sometimes use this as a reason for refusing to consider a woman candidate. To do so, they argue, may threaten the unity of the church, resulting in a loss of membership and income.

An encouraging trend among the American Baptists is the increase in the number of women attending their seminaries. In 1975–76 women comprised 14 percent of the total student body. By 1978–79 that proportion had risen to 23 percent. A survey conducted by the denomination revealed that only about two-thirds of the women graduates actually seek ministerial positions. Of those seeking such positions, about 72 percent are able to find an appointment. This suggests considerable openness on the part of congregations to accepting women as ministers.

A closer analysis of the figures, however, revealed that of those women entering the ministry, only 79 percent were placed in a church. A comparative sampling of men indicated that 99 percent of the male graduates seeking ministerial positions were so placed. The seminary women were sometimes diverted to child-care centers, social agencies, schools, and counseling. In addition, while 67 percent of the men placed in churches occupied the position of "pastor," only 30 percent of the women assumed that title. Moreover, the average salary of the men was $2,000 higher than that of the women, and their allowances for travel, conferences, and other expenses were double that granted to the women. While most of the men were ordained either before or immediately after graduation, it was not unusual for women to wait two or more years before receiving ordination.

On the basis of such findings, members of the "Study of Women in Ministry" survey made a number of recommendations aimed at improving the status of women ministers within the American Baptist Church. Seminaries were requested to enhance the opportunities for women with respect to recruitment, degree expectations, financial aid, field experience, and placement possibilities. Congregations were exhorted to encourage women as well as men to respond to the call to ministry. Local churches were requested to include women in all offices, and pulpit committees were to search out information on women candidates. It was recommended that scholarship funds be made available for women ministerial candidates and that the recipients be utilized as speakers at churches, conferences, and state conventions. Because pastoral leadership is a significant influencing factor, ministers were requested to educate congregations toward the acceptance of women as pastors, and to encourage and welcome women pastors in the community. It was recommended that executive and area ministers employ competent women at all staff levels and that they act as advocates for women seeking placement.

These recommendations are now being worked out within the

structure of the American Baptist Church. The study group concluded its investigation with this statement:

> Our conviction is that the ministry will grow in effectiveness and the church will better fulfill its mission if churches, laity, ministers and executives accept women and men equally as ministers.[30]

The Southern Baptist Convention

The Southern Baptist Convention has only recently entered into dialogue concerning the ordination of women. No resolution on this issue has been passed by the Southern Baptists. One was once proposed but was ruled out of order on the basis that it was not appropriate business for the convention. There are no requirements laid down by the S.B.C. concerning ministerial appointments. A person may be ordained to ministry with a minimum of educational qualifications and with little or no experience if a local church so chooses. As there are no specific guidelines for the ordination of ministers in general, it is argued that no statement concerning the sex of an ordination candidate is called for. Consequently churches tend to be guided in this area by unwritten but longstanding tradition.

This tradition has evolved out of an economic and cultural milieu in which women were relegated to positions of lesser honor than those occupied by men. They were, however, required to be actively involved in the church, so that for generations women have provided the backbone of Southern Baptist mission outreach, Christian education, and so on. Yet they have not received the recognition accorded to men in titles of honor and financial remuneration. In many Southern Baptist churches it will be maintained that women are "thought of very highly," but they are frequently relegated to positions in which they have little participation in decision-making or in the leading of community worship.

Although the S.B.C. has not specifically addressed the matter of the ordination of women, it has passed two resolutions in the last decade which relate indirectly to the issue. Both reflect the deeply ingrained attitudes toward women which characterize many Southern Baptist congregations. The most recent resolution, passed by the 1980 convention, states that the S.B.C. does not endorse the Equal Rights Amendment. An earlier resolution, approved by the 1973 convention, took the form of a somewhat vague statement entitled, "On the Place of Women in Christian Service."[31] This resolution makes reference to "the distinctive roles of men and women in the church and in the home," suggests that mission promotion and education are spheres of service suitable for women, and claims that "most women's liberation movements" are attacking what the S.B.C. defines as the "scriptural precepts of woman's place in society." The resolution states that the Bible is "explicitly clear" on this subject. Reference is made to "God's order of authority," namely, Christ the head of every man, man the head of the woman, and children in subjection to parents. Attention is drawn to the fact that man was not made for the woman but the woman for the man, though they are dependent on one another.

The resolution does not make clear why mission promotion (evangelism) and education (teaching) are ministries open to women, while (by implication) the pastorate is not. If the S.B.C. is taking seriously the literalist interpretation of the scriptural guidelines, then the "I permit no woman to teach" (1 Tim. 2.12) controversy has evidently been overlooked. If, however, the S.B.C. is aware, from a study of Scripture, that women were participating in preaching and teaching ministries in the early Christian communities, it is hard to understand why this body would exclude women from these same ministries within the context of the pastorate of the local church. Furthermore, although the Pauline statement concerning the interdependence of man and woman (1 Cor. 11:8-12) is referred to, no attempt is made to come to terms with the new insight that it portrays concerning the status of women.

In the absence of any competent exegetical statement from the national leadership of the church, Southern Baptist congregations have sought to grapple with the matter on an individual basis. In 1976, for example, twenty-five-year-old Suzanne Coyle requested to be ordained by her home church. Coyle had grown up in Gravel Switch, Kentucky, where she had attended Beech Fork Baptist Church regularly and had played the piano for its worship services. She was graduated from Center College in Danville, Kentucky, and earned a Master of Divinity degree in Pastoral Theology from Princeton Theological Seminary. On the basis of her outstanding work at Princeton, Coyle was awarded a scholarship for post-graduate studies. Since her early college days, however, she had felt called to the ministry. At the time of her ordination request she was employed by the Southern Baptist Home Mission Board and was working as chaplain-pastor of Central City Baptist Chapel, Philadelphia. After consultation with Coyle, the deacons of Beech Fork were convinced that God had called her to the ministry and that she should be recommended for ordination. On December 6, 1976, the congregation voted to ordain her.

Coyle's ordination took place in February, 1977. In April of that year the South District Association registered its disapproval. Beech Fork Baptist Church was notified that if it did not rescind Coyle's ordination, the executive board of the South District Association would recommend that the church be withdrawn from fellowship. By the time the annual meeting of this body was held in October, it was clear that Beech Fork was not willing to rescind the ordination. By a vote of 98 to 64 this congregation was therefore excluded from the fellowship of the South District Association.

The issue of the ordination of women is also raised from time to time at the state level. At the Kentucky State Convention held in November, 1977, a pastor attempted to introduce a resolution opposing the ordination of women. This was rejected. Instead, a "Resolution of Ordination" was passed which reads as follows:

BE IT RESOLVED,

1. That the place of authority for ordination is centered in the authority of the local church under the authority of scripture. Churches ordain. Conventions do not.
2. That the recognition of the ordination and the utilization of those thus ordained is also the prerogative of the local church.

This resolution at least permits local churches the freedom to decide which individuals meet the biblical requirements for ordination, whether those individuals be male or female. Individual autonomy is, as the resolution indicates, in accordance with common practice in Southern Baptist churches.

In September, 1978, a "Consultation on Women in Church Related Vocations" was held in Nashville, Tennessee—the first national consultation of its kind for this denomination. In attendance were 295 persons representing 25 states. Catherine Allen of the Women's Missionary Union was chairperson, and in her opening address she called for a more honest approach in confronting women and girls with the challenge of professional service within the denomination. "We must stop dangling terms such as freedom, life commitment, call of God, priesthood of the believer, personal accountability, and church related vocations before their cars, eyes and noses if they are not supposed to hear, see and appropriate them."[32] The purpose of the consultation was to explore such issues in the presence of those persons who are most influential in establishing policies and in educating congregations. Only about five hundred copies of the document containing the findings of this consultation have been made available for circulation.

At present there are about 55,000 ministers in the Southern Baptist Convention, of whom about 33,000 are ordained and acting as pastors. Ordination is not a prerequisite for a pastoral appointment, but it has certain legal implications. Apart from the tax break for which it qualifies one, it enables the individual to perform services such as wedding ceremonies. Although official statistics are not readily available, it appears that at present there are only about one hundred ordained women in the Southern Baptist Convention.

There are many other women "in ministry," but they are not ordained. Chaplaincy appointments are more common for women than pastoral appointments, and because the military chaplaincy requires ordination, the Chaplaincy Division of the Home Missions Board has been authorized to ordain women. There are apparently large numbers of women in S.B.C. seminaries who would like to be ordained, but few of these women expect to find pastorates. Some Southern Baptist churches will not even consider women for ordination as deacons.

In the absence of hierarchical control, the key to this situation is probably in the hands of the seminaries. Careful exegesis of Scripture, the elimination of prejudice, and sensitivity to issues relating to sexism would equip new church leaders with the ability to assign more equitably the varied ministries that God has given the church. In the meantime, the Christian Life Commission assumes responsibility for matters of a moral and ethical nature, and it is this body which is giving visibility to the issues relating to women in the Southern Baptist Convention.[33]

Christian Church (Disciples of Christ)

Throughout its long history the Christian Church (Disciples of Christ) has ordained women to the ministry as missionaries and as parish ministers. In the early 1970s, however, this denomination showed great concern over the fact that comparatively few women were actively involved within the leadership structure of the church. The 1973 yearbook revealed that only 4 percent of professional church workers were women, less than 9 percent of the church's seminarians were women, and women were inadequately represented at the executive level of the church. Very few churches had women elders, and although women featured in the diaconate of a number of churches, the existence of separate boards of deacons and deaconesses often reflected a devaluation of the serving ministry of women.

The General Assembly of the Christian Church (Disciples of

Christ), meeting in Cincinnati, Ohio, October, 1973, passed resolutions geared to changing this situation. It was recommended that a single order of the diaconate be implemented, representing men and women equally. All the bodies of the church were requested to be aggressive in the recruitment of women for preparation for professional church vocations. A high priority was to be given to the provision of financial support for such women. In order to redress the balance at the executive level, it was recommended that men should be considered for vacant positions only if no competent women could be found. Congregations which had called women as pastors were commended, and other congregations were encouraged to follow their example.

Resolution 37 of the assembly was concerned specifically with women in ministry. It was observed that women ministers in the Christian Church (Disciples of Christ) did not receive equal treatment with men in recruitment, in education, in placement, or in financial remuneration. Such discrimination, though unintentional, was depriving the church of balance in the appeal and effectiveness of the gospel. It was therefore resolved that women be encouraged to commit themselves to the full-time vocation of ministry in word and sacrament. Women were to be given equal consideration for pastorates and in the staffing of other significant positions. The Equal Rights Amendment was strongly endorsed, and it was specified that within the Christian Church (Disciples of Christ) women should receive equal remuneration for equal vocational tasks.

The year 1974 marked the centennial of the founding of the first national organization of women—the Christian Women's Board of Missions. In 1920 this board joined with the American Christian Missionary Society to form the United Christian Missionary Society. This body is the primary programing and outreach unit of the church. At the time of its foundation it was agreed that the governing board would be comprised equally of men and women. The UCMS has provided a healthy example for the other agencies within the church. Much of the present increase in the participation of women in the church is due to its influence. Women are now serving on all the governing boards of the major units of the church and on all the regional boards. Percentages range from 12 percent to 50 percent. In 1980 the Church Finance Council, which collects and distributes all finances for the entire denomination, had a woman serving as president.

The Christian Church (Disciples of Christ) is actively conducting seminars enabling women to function more fully as decision-makers in the church. These seminars are being attended by women in all thirty-five regions of the denomination throughout the United States and Canada. Seminars concerning the diaconate and the eldership are also being conducted. These lay positions are extremely important in the guidance and functioning of congregational life, and until very recently women were almost entirely excluded from both of these offices. This is no longer the case; women are now functioning in both of these offices in increasing numbers. Guidelines concerning the inclusive use of language in worship are being made available for the use of church leaders.

The American Lutheran Church; the Lutheran Church in America; and the Lutheran Church—Missouri Synod

These Lutheran churches, although organized separately at this present time, are all members of the Lutheran Council of the U.S.A. and have much in common with one another. They do differ, however, on the matter of the ordination of women, the Lutheran Church—Missouri Synod being opposed to it.

In 1972 *The American Lutheran Church* produced a brief document entitled, "Women and Men in Church and Society—Towards Wholeness in the Christian Community." While affirming the "profound mystery" of God-given sexuality "which both separates and attracts us," the statement challenges the sex-stereotyping which pervades Western culture. Qualities such as gentleness, compassion, helpfulness, and artistic appreciation are found to varying degrees in both males and females, as are qualities of assertiveness, vigor, initiative, and strength. All human beings are created in God's image, and the mystery of femaleness and maleness is to be celebrated as one of God's gifts.

It is not necessary, the statement maintains, for men and women to view one another as antagonists. It is human estrangement from God which gives birth to insecurity and which leads to competition, conflict, fear, and the abuse of power. In the family and in social life the roles of men and women are changing. Christians must come to terms with the true nature of personhood. Neither marriage nor parenthood are indicators of personal worth. Sexuality is a part of life, but it is not the whole of life. "Men and women are equal as persons, complementary in their sexuality, mutually related in their wholeness."

In this statement the American Lutheran Church confesses that in the past it has tended to accept the ways of society as though they were the ways of God. A reexamination of the Scriptures, however, has convinced the church leadership that it has been in error. The Scriptures do not forbid the ordination of women or their service in the ministry of Word and sacrament, nor do they consign women to a subordinate role in the church.

The implications of this are far-reaching. Nominating committees are exhorted to take active steps to bring women into leadership roles in the church. Care is to be taken to eliminate from constitutions, worship forms, and official statements any pronouns or expressions that would deny to women their full participation in the life of the church. Editors of church publications are to guard against the perpetration of stereotypes that would artificially limit the choices open to men and to women. Seminary faculties are requested to be active in encouraging women to pursue theological education. Specifically, they are to appoint women to seminary teaching positions and to create an acceptable climate for women seminarians.

The church's concern for the personhood of each man and woman is also to be reflected at the congregational level. Congregations are to be encouraged to demonstrate their acceptance of ordained women; both laymen and laywomen are to be involved in ministry roles whenever the church assembles for study or worship or participation in the sacraments. Informal group meetings are to explore issues relating to human roles as an aid toward communication and understanding. Outside the church, concerted efforts should be made to protest the distorted sexuality and sexual stereotypes featured in the mass media. Within the church, congregations should strive for equal opportunities with respect to service, advancement, and reward for all their employees.

These trends are comparatively recent. At present only 70 of the 5,800 ordained pastors in the American Lutheran Church are women. This figure is expected to increase significantly in the near future. In the four seminaries listed by the denomination, the collective enrollment of students studying full-time in the Master of Divinity programs during 1979 was reported as consisting of 866 men and 131 women. Many of these women will no doubt be ordained as ministers. The vast majority of women presently involved in the leadership of the American Lutheran church are lay staff, and there are many hundreds of these.

The *Lutheran Church in America* is also now working actively to encourage the inclusion and support of women in professional leadership roles. A handbook is being produced to aid call committees in filling congregational vacancies. These committees are being encouraged to examine possibilities for the placement of women. In the nine seminaries listed for the denomination, curriculum changes are being encouraged to strengthen education relative to women in ministry. Strategies are being devised to improve campus climate and to provide a supply of qualified women who may be appointed to the faculties. During 1978, the candidates enrolled in the Master of Divinity program numbered 1,077, of whom 236 were women. More than 90 women are ordained as ministers in the Lutheran

Church in America. The denomination is calling for women writers and book reviewers for its journal, *Partners;* and it has expressed an openness to consider any specific goals, objectives, or strategies which might strengthen the support of women in the professional leadership of the church.

The *Lutheran Church—Missouri Synod* has been concerned over the past decade with the matter of granting women suffrage. It was not until 1969 that women in this denomination were given "permission to vote in their local congregations, to serve as delegates to District and Synodical conventions, and to hold elective or appointive positions on District and Synodical boards and commissions."[34] The 1969 convention in Denver declared that, "Those statements of Scripture which direct women to keep silent in the church and which prohibit them to teach and to exercise authority over men, we understand to mean that women ought not to hold the pastoral office." The resolution continues, "We hold that they do not prohibit full membership of women on synodical boards, commissions, and committees"; and "We hold likewise that Scripture does not prohibit women from exercising the franchise in congregational or synodical assemblies."[35]

The Synod and the congregations of the Synod were on this basis given the freedom to adjust their policies and practices relating to the involvement of women in the church. In 1972, the Commission on Theology and Church Relations endorsed this statement, urging members of the Synod "to recognize the right of each congregation to judge according to its circumstances whether it is necessary or expedient for it to introduce woman suffrage."[36] In the meantime, the 1971 convention had adopted a resolution, "To withhold ordination of women to the pastoral office." This resolution quoted from the proceedings of the Denver convention as they related to the pastoral office and resolved "that the Synod reaffirm its position that the Word of God does not permit women to hold the pastoral office or serve in any capacity involving distinctive functions of this office." The "distinctive functions of this office" would include preaching, the public administration of the sacraments, and church discipline.

Data gathered by a Task Force on Women in 1975 indicated that 64 percent of the congregations participating in its survey had implemented the 1969 resolution. However, the number of women in leadership positions in these churches was still very low. In most congregations women were excluded from assuming the position of president, vice-president, or elder. Many congregations appeared satisfied with the more traditional roles for women, such as secretaries, choir directors, organists, and teachers of Bible classes for women. At the district and synodical levels women were still by and large excluded from the decision-making processes of the church.

The Task Force on Women reported that similar discrimination was identified in the educational sphere. For example, out of the districts reporting, only 4 percent of the elementary school principals were women, and almost without exception women teachers were receiving a substantially lower median salary than their male counterparts. In the Synod's colleges, of sixty-eight persons holding the rank of full professor, only one was a woman. Equal percentages of men and women and essentially equal salaries were found only at the instructor level.

In view of the fact that 54 percent of the Synod's communicant membership is female, the Task Force on Women recognized that tremendous resources and talents available to the church are not at present being utilized. It advocated continuing study on the role of women in the church. And in view of the fact that "the concept of ministry is changing from an authority figure to a servanthood model,"[37] the task force recommended that the Commission on Theology and Church Relations should focus attention on studies relating to the meaning of ordination. In particular it should study the relationship of ministry and the priesthood of believers to the office of pastor, the question of women serving as pastors, the male/female qualities ascribed to God, and male/female relationships and roles as outlined in the Scriptures. The fact that this frightens or bewilders some people should not deter the church from its endeavor to affirm and strengthen the ministry of women within its congregations.

The United Methodist Church

The Methodist church has from its earliest days licensed women to preach, but it was not until 1956 that there was an official removal of all ordination restrictions based on sex. In that year the General Conference voted "full clergy rights for women." The United Methodist church came into being in 1968 when the Evangelical United Brethren church and the Methodist church united. At that time women received guaranteed annual appointment by the bishop, involving either a pastoral charge or a special appointment beyond the local church. From that time onward the United Methodist church has endeavored to be supportive of women clergy.

Legislation was enacted at the 1976 General Conference affirming the need for an educated and informed professional ministry. The conference clearly stated its desire to unite theory and practice with respect to women ministers.

In the same year, the Women's Division published a policy statement entitled, "Ministries to Women and Ministries to Children." In this statement the observation is made that when the Methodist church came into being, prejudice and the limitations of cultural attitudes precluded women from assuming significant roles within the church. Even now, after many years of struggle, it is often true that the status of women in the church, as in society, is frequently tied to sex-stereotyped roles. "We believe," the policy statement reads, "that the church is still in captivity to male values, structures, and practices and consequently is unable to be the locus of genuine community."

The Women's Division maintains in this statement that the cultural norm concerning women, both in the United States and overseas, is antithetical to the gospel and should be challenged. Women should be freed from the captivity in which they have so long been held. This liberation is "an imperative out of the heart of the Gospel, and where it is in evidence, is the working of the Holy Spirit." The statement recommends that programs be devised which enable women to participate fully at all levels of decision-making in the church; that women be given opportunity to develop leadership potential and to serve on governing boards and in executive leadership; and that a more aggressive program of recruitment of women for all forms of the ministry be initiated. Men should be trained to confront and deal with "the nature, scope and effect of discrimination and prejudice within this world of difficult choices and conflicting values."

In 1978, United Methodist women participated actively in a campaign to extend the deadline for ratification of the Equal Rights Amendment to the Constitution. The Women's Division also sponsored an Equal Rights Amendment Inquiry in North Carolina and in Oklahoma, two of the fifteen states which had not at the time ratified the amendment. The Commission on the Status and Role of Women (mandated by the 1972 General Conference) planned regional events geared toward increasing the number of women delegates to the 1980 General Conference. Women's issues were given greater prominence throughout the denomination.

There are, at this present time, more than one thousand ordained women ministering within the United Methodist church. The first major study of these clergywomen was published in 1980. It is entitled *New Witnesses* and is authored by Harry Hale, Morton King, and Doris Moreland Jones. This study focuses on the dramatic increase in the number of women clergy in recent years, and it analyzes the problems and possibilities inherent in this situation.

In spite of initial difficulties the study group had in obtaining a list of these ordained women, the eventual participation in the project was unusually high—more than 90 percent of those listed responded to questionnaires. A startling number of these were ordained between 1968 and 1980. They had transferred directly from college to seminary to ministerial positions. Sixty-two percent of the women were under forty years of age. (The mean age for all clergy was 45.1 years.) Of the women elders, 50 percent were ordained in the three-year period preceding the study. In 1979, 87 percent of the women were serving in local churches rather than in special ministries, 67 percent of these being pastors in charge of a local congregation.

The United Methodist church elected its first woman bishop on July 17, 1980. Marjorie Swank Matthews is a native of Onaway, Michigan, where she served the church as a layperson for many years. After her ordination, she held pastorates in New York, Florida, and Georgia, and was a member of the cabinet of the conference for five years. Bishop Matthews was elected to the highest office of the church at the North Central Jurisdictional conference in Dayton, Ohio. A 460-delegate assembly voted her into the office of bishop by acclamation and with overwhelming enthusiasm. She is now bishop of the Wisconsin Area of the church and leader of the 140,000 United Methodists who fall under her jurisdiction. Part of her duty as bishop is to ordain men and women who desire to become clergy.

The situation relating to women in the United Methodist church is thus encouraging in many areas. However, there are still obstacles to be overcome. Self-doubt sometimes plagues women seminarians who feel called to ministry. It is often easier for a woman to declare herself for diaconal ministry than to seek ordination as an elder. In the diaconate a woman may serve in such areas as Christian education, church music, and church communications—roles more acceptable to the community at large. Some pastors are reluctant to receive female candidates for membership in annual conferences. A woman who experiences a sincere call to ordained ministry but receives no affirmation from the church may very likely abandon her vocation. Such a frustrating experience may lead to psychological disturbance and may cause the person to leave the church in anger or bitterness. Energies which could be better channeled into church ministry are sometimes dissipated in defending a call. So there are still barriers to be broken down.

The United Presbyterian Church, U.S.A. and the Presbyterian Church, U.S.

The *United Presbyterian Church, U.S.A.* is by far the largest single body of Presbyterians in the United States. It came into being in 1958 when the Presbyterian Church in the U.S.A. merged with the United Presbyterian Church of North America. In the early years of this church's history, women struggled to receive recognition as preachers and as ordained ministers. In 1912, a woman was licensed to preach, but this license was revoked one year later. It was not until 1930, after much debate, that the General Assembly approved the ordination of women to the office of elder (a lay office), specifying that personal pronouns used in the regulations relating to ruling elders "should be interpreted generically, that is, as applying to either men or women."[38] In 1956—a quarter of a century later—the General Assembly of the United Presbyterian Church, U.S.A. approved the ordination of women to the ministry of sacrament and Word, stating that "both men and women may be called to this office."[39]

The opportunity thus provided did not result in an overwhelming influx of women into ministerial positions. By 1971, only 103 women were listed as ordained clergy in the United Presbyterian Church, U.S.A. Since that time, however, there has been a rapid increase in these numbers. In 1978, 410 women were so listed out of a total ministerial force numbering around 14,000. This number of women ministers is expected to escalate. Presbyterian seminaries report dramatic increases in the number of women enrolled in Master of Divinity programs. From 1977 to 1978, for example, this grouping nearly doubled, rising from 343 to 600. Women seeking ordination, however, continue to experience resistance. Indeed some churches, as recently as 1978, were not even willing to appoint women elders.

In order to facilitate change in attitudes and to assist in the placement of women in professional ministries, the denomination has embarked on a five-year project in which the problems are being systematically approached. One publication resulting from this is the *Resource Book for Placement, Acceptance and Support of Clergywomen,* written by Penelope Colman and Ann Conrad. Strategies have been defined in the areas of suasion, education, and visibility. Simple, clear, direct models have been produced in each of these areas defining activities, goals, and long-range objectives which could be adapted to any church situation. Included in this publication is a short study contributed by Roberta Hestenes, an ordained minister in the United Presbyterian Church, entitled "Scripture and the Ministry of Women Within the Christian Community." After careful study of the issues involved, Hestenes concludes, "The choice we today are faced with seems to be whether or not to move forward towards God's ultimate purpose or to remain mired in the past and fearful of change" (p. 37).

This particular church, it seems, is continuing to move forward. The 1980 General Assembly decided that the appointment of women as elders was no longer to be optional. Each congregation is now required to ordain both men and women as elders. Any church which finds itself unable to abide by this rule must write to the Presbytery giving reasons for its inability to conform and requesting permission to appoint only men. The Presbytery must accept the reasons as being valid by a two-thirds vote. The Vocation Agency has produced a 16mm film entitled "A New Wave Breaking: Women Are Ministers," which recreates the story of a nominating committee which called a woman to the pastorate of its church. A study guide has been produced to help viewers analyze and assess their own thinking on the issues with which the film deals.[40]

The *Presbyterian Church, U.S.* is in formal relationship with the

United Presbyterian Church, U.S.A. and shares many of the same attitudes in relation to the ministry of women. The 119th General Assembly (1979) agreed that whenever a joint U.P.C./P.C.U.S. General Assembly is held, it will meet only in a state which has ratified the Equal Rights Amendment. In anticipation of a future merger, a Joint Committee on Women has been established to develop plans for united programs and organizations.

The present Committee on Women's Concerns of this denomination came into being in 1972, when the Board of Women's Work was integrated during the restructuring of Assembly agencies. The committee is responsible for the development of national strategy, for voicing the concerns of women, and for the promotion of increased responsiveness in the church toward the resources of women. In particular the Committee on Women's Concerns works toward a more equitable representation of women in all church courts and their committees, boards, and agencies. As yet this is still way below desirable levels. The committee estimates that at the present rate of progress it will take another seventeen years to raise the representation of women as church officers to 33 percent, and another thirty-four years to raise this to 50 percent. Only when this time comes will the church operating structure realistically represent the proportion of women in the church.

In the 1978 General Assembly, the Presbyterian Church, U.S. elected its first woman moderator, Sara B. Moseley. At this assembly, the Committee on Women's Concerns recommended, among other things, that the Book of Church Order be edited to ensure that inclusive language is being used. All 485 of the noninclusive terms which feature in the 1977-78 edition of this book are to be changed in time for the next printing or no later than 1983. Presbyterian Church, U.S. seminaries registered 146 women during the 1978-79 academic year among the 1,010 students enrolled for the first professional degree. At this time about 145 of the approximately 5,431 people ordained and in pastoral ministry in the Presbyterian Church, U.S. are women.

Conclusions

It is evident that there are encouraging trends in many branches of the church. New perspectives gained from the study of Scripture and from reflection on the course of history are being translated into concrete realities. Some churches are still in the initial stages of investigation, organizing conferences and informal study groups which focus on women in ministry. Other churches have moved beyond this to definite legislation which grants women equal status with men in church leadership. But for all churches there are still issues to be addressed. In particular there is the need to continue to search out ways to actualize in the local churches ideals which are written into state or national church constitutions. Ministers and seminary faculty are the people who have the most influence in this area. To ministers belongs the task of educating congregations and implementing policies. To seminary faculty falls the responsibility of so training future ministers that they will be competent to redress the balance of ministerial function as they enter the sphere of the local church.

Notes

[1] Constance J. Tarasal and Irina Kirillova, eds., *Orthodox Women: Their Role and Participation in the Orthodox Church* (Geneva, Switzerland: WCC, 1977), p. 17. Printed in the USA by Office Assistance Inc.

[2] Ibid., p. 19.

[3] Ibid., p. 20-22.

[4] Ibid., p. 21.

[5] Ibid., p. 27.

[6] Ibid., p. 28.

[7] Ibid.

[8] Statement written by Franjo Cardinal Seper and Father Jérôme Hamer. Approved by Paul VI (London: Catholic Truth Society, 1976). The text is contained in *The Order of Priesthood* (Huntington, Ind.: Our Sunday Visitor, 1978), pp. 1-20.

[9] "Every type of discrimination, whether social or cultural, whether based on sex, race, color, social condition, language, or religion, is to be overcome and eradicated as contrary to God's intent. For in truth, it must still be regretted that fundamental personal rights are not yet being universally honored. Such is the case of a woman who is denied the right and freedom to choose a husband, to embrace a state of life, or to acquire an education or cultural benefits equal to those recognised

for men." *The Church Today*, p. 29, in The Documents of Vatican II, ed. W. M. Abbott (New York: Corpus, 1966), pp. 227–28.

[10]*The Order of Priesthood*, p. 3.

[11]Ibid., p. 4.

[12]Ibid.

[13]Ibid., p. 10.

[14]Ibid., p. 12.

[15]See *Women and Catholic Priesthood: The Detroit Ordination Conference, 1975*, ed. Anne Marie Gardiner (New York: Paulist, 1976). This book contains an excellent bibliography, pp. 199–208.

[16]Ibid., p. 19.

[17]Ibid., p. 31.

[18]Ibid., pp. 66–88.

[19]Ibid., p. 91.

[20]Ibid., p. 73.

[21]Ibid., p. 122.

[22]Ibid., pp. 255–257.

[23]*Catholic Biblical Quarterly* 41 (1979): 608–13.

[24]Ibid., p. 611.

[25]Ibid., p. 613.

[26]Fran Ferder, *Called to Break Bread?* (Mt. Ranier, Mich.: Quixote Centre, 1978).

[27]Ibid., p. 11.

[28]Bylaws, Article VII, Section 2.K, as quoted in "Does God Deny Spiritual Manifestations and Ministry Gifts to Women?" Joseph R. Flower, General Secretary, General Council of the Assemblies of God, January 2, 1978 (unpublished).

[29]*A Study of Women in Ministry*, E. C. Lehman and the Task Force on Women in Ministry of the Ministers' Council, American Baptist Churches, 1979.

[30]Ibid., p. 91.

[31]Resolution No. 12, Annual of the S.B.C., 1973.

[32]*Findings of the Consultation on Women in Church-Related Vocations*, p. 6.

[33]See Leon McBeth, *Women in Baptist Life* (Nashville: Broadman, 1979).

[34]*Convention Workbook 1975*, p. 58.

[35]*Convention Proceedings 1969*, Resolution 2, p. 17.

[36]*Convention Workbook 1973*, Appendix A, pp. 37–38.

[37]*Convention Workbook 1977*, p. 54.

[38]*Digest of the Acts and Deliberances of the General Assembly of the Presbyterian Church in the U.S.A.*, Vol. 1 (Philadelphia: 1938), p. 462.

[39]*The Book of Order*, Part II, Form of Government, chapter 8, Sec. 2,38.02.

[40]See Elizabeth Verdesi, *In But Still Out* (Philadelphia: Westminster, 1973).

WOMEN
IN SEMINARY

SEMINARIES AND DIVINITY schools throughout the United States are training church leaders of tomorrow. Attitudes toward women which they encourage are likely to be reflected in the churches which their graduates later serve. These attitudes find expression on a theoretical level, in curriculum content, and on a practical level in the way in which women seminarians are treated. This chapter gives insight into the present experience of a random sample of women seminarians.

A dramatic increase has been reported in the number of women enrolled in seminary and divinity school programs. Many of these women are not content to be channeled into traditional roles but are studying along with men in disciplines leading to the Master of Divinity, Doctor of Ministry, or Doctor of Philosophy degrees. They are thus earning qualifications which lead directly into the field of church leadership. Do these women embark on advanced training with a strong sense of call to ministry? Do the seminaries and divinity schools generally support women students by affirming their commitment and preparing them for leadership? How do these women handle problem situations, and what advice would they give to others contemplating professional service within the church? In order to search out information on issues such as these, questionnaires were circulated to a limited number of schools across the United States. In response, many women wrote at length about their motivation for entering theological schools and about their experience of study, worship, and service within these communities. The information contained in this chapter has been asssembled directly from these questionnaires. Although they are not equally representative of all denominations, they do provide an honest insight into the issues faced by women anticipating professional church ministry.[1]

Call to Ministry

The sense of call experienced by these women was, as one would expect, similar in most respects to that commonly known to be experienced by men aspiring to Christian ministry. Many had felt from early childhood a strong desire to participate in church leadership, and some could look back to a specific moment when they became significantly aware of their destiny. A first-year student at Gordon-Conwell Theological Seminary wrote, "I recognized this call as an elementary school child, playing 'minister,' dreaming of going to the Congo or pastoring a church (although my parents are not overtly religious)." And a graduating senior from the Jesuit School of Theology at Berkeley recalled this memorable childhood experience: "At age eight, in a Catholic May procession, I had a powerful sense of being called. This call was nurtured through communication with strong women religious during my grade and high school years. They taught me to deepen in spirituality, to listen in faith, to believe in my giftedness, to name and claim my Christian heritage, to trust my God experiences."

For some, the sense of call came to fruition only after they had already embarked on training for other careers and in some cases after many years of work in secular professions. One seminarian wrote, "I always had a sneaking suspicion that this was what I would like to do, but it was not until I had experienced approximately twenty years in the business world that I decided that now was the time for me to make a change." Another was drawn toward Christian ministry after training and experience in secular journalism. She became aware of the poor quality of much of the religious press in the United States and felt considerable unease until she applied to seminary. She hopes to direct her call to ministry through literature rather than through the pastorate. A second-year seminarian wrote, "I believe that God calls all of us according to how we as individuals can best hear him. For me it was an increasing dissatisfaction with a career that I had at one time thoroughly enjoyed coupled with a hunger to know God more intimately and to serve him by entering a full-time Christian vocation." Another ministerial candidate had spent fifteen years as a public school teacher before beginning seminary training. Her sense of call came about as a result of reading certain articles concerning women in ministry. "When I would read an article about women in the ministry, I would feel a definite push in that direction . . . it seemed a little unreal or impossible at first, but the assurances after reading Scripture and praying outweighed all doubts."

Other seminarians have been drawn gradually toward ordination through active involvement in Christian leadership. Practical experience in a ministerial setting provided for them the guidance needed to direct them into professional training. This kind of experience was common: "I was head of our youth group while in high school, and because we were without a youth director, I became one. To see the way God could use me really influenced my decision to enter the ministry." A second-year student at Fuller Theological Seminary observed, "Field education experiences as hospital chaplain and assistant pastor have shown me not only that I enjoy the ministry but that I can effectively minister." And a first-year student at the Theological School, Drew University, wrote, "I am ruling elder, Sunday school teacher, Bethel adult education teacher, Christian education chairman, worship committee chairman, and have been elected to attend the General Assembly in the

United Presbyterian Church. Throughout all my eight years of involvement, I have felt a growing desire to enter the ministry in a professional sense so that I could reach more people in a different way."

Happy are those who find in their home church an environment which nurtures the leadership potential of both men and women. A student from Bethel Theological Seminary wrote highly of her home church: "Gifts of leadership were really developed here. My pastor gave me every opportunity to function—from in the pulpit, to committees, to financial help through college and seminary." Other women, however, have been less fortunate. One seminarian wrote, "My home church supported me when I was planning to pursue youth work as a career. Now that I hope to do doctoral work, my pastor hardly acknowledges my presence when I go home." And another commented, "My home church has helped support me financially, but it places me in a secondary position to the boys in the church who want to go into church work, even if they are in junior high school." This kind of discrimination was commonly experienced: "When the deacons decided to license two young men who had made public commitments to preach, I was the subject of much debate. Several men were adamant that I not be overlooked. The final outcome—a homemade certificate proclaiming 'to all men [sic!] our encouragement and prayerful support of her,' but not so bold a step as licensing."

Women entering seminary later in life have a similar problem: "When I decided to quit my job and go to seminary, the church had a rather ho-hum attitude ('another restless housewife'). When my forty-year-old male counterpart does the same—this is a highly praised and sacrificial act." Some churches communicate a confusing message to the women of their congregations. A first-year doctoral student wrote, "My home church was very frustrating. On one hand they acknowledged my gifts, on the other they forbade or blocked their usage." Sometimes churches will manipulate a situation by subtly channeling gifted women into areas of service more culturally acceptable: "My home church has affirmed my teaching abilities but has discouraged me from seeking the pastorate."

Unhappily, such tactics are sometimes employed even in the seminary arena. Women who have entered seminary with the intention of training for the pastorate find that at this stage in their career it is easy to become sidetracked. Women seminarians discover very quickly that they are affirmed when they indicate a calling toward areas of service which parallel those assigned to the female by Western culture, while they are gently discouraged when they indicate that they have other goals. Because people, whether male or female, need the strength that a supportive community gives, there is a strong tendency for women seminarians to move into these other spheres of service in order to gain approbation and acceptance. Many find that they must consciously grapple with this gravitational pull. They must learn to distinguish between those tasks for which God has equipped them and to which he is calling them and those tasks to which others might wish to conveniently assign then.

It takes courage to cross culturally established boundaries. A student from Duke Divinity School wrote, "For awhile I sought to ignore my call to the pastorate, seeking instead to serve God in other areas, such as counseling. By the time I reached my last year of college, I knew that I had to go into the ministry. At first I said 'yes' to the call if I didn't have to preach, but that no longer stands. I know that I have been called to pastor a local congregation in all areas of responsibilities and duties, particularly in preaching." Another student wrote, "I entered divinity school planning on teaching. I never thought at all of going into the parish ministry until I came into contact with other women who were going into it. I began to realize that the church needed women in its ordained ministry. I first heard my call the first time I preached."

A student from Trinity Evangelical Divinity School struggled with the same issues: "I have felt drawn to full-time Christian work since the time I made a personal commitment to Christ in high school. I have considered meeting this through para-church work, overseas missions, or through being a pastor's wife. I never considered the pastoral ministry myself because I had always been taught that this would be against the teaching of Scripture." This student reported that a careful study of Scripture during her seminary training convinced her that she had been mistaken in these views and that as a woman and a Christian she was indeed free to participate fully and equally in church leadership. She and her husband are now anticipating a team ministry in which they share equally in mutual submission to one another. Patricia Gundry's book, *Woman Be Free* (Zondervan, 1979), was especially helpful to her in reaching these conclusions.

The Hebrew Scriptures provide many examples of people who struggled with the reality of their call to the service of God and the nature of that call. Women seminarians also struggle. Behind them is a long tradition of the suppression of women's gifts, and surrounding them sometimes is an atmosphere of questioning and suspicion. With few role models and much conflicting exegesis, women often fight a lonely battle. Some, however, find that they are not alone and that others are struggling with them. A Fuller seminarian observed, "My understanding of my call has grown out of a long and often painful struggle within myself as to whether women can be called to be pastors. I was helped tremendously . . . by my husband, by professors, by friends, and by my own pastor." From Pacific School of Religion, a fourth-year student wrote, "I still have many questions about the validity of work as an ordained pastor, but I continue going toward that because it seems the best way, or the only way right now, to continue my call to serve." And a third-year student from Southern Baptist Theological Seminary commented, "My 'call' became more refined as I entered seminary and began to get a glimpse of my talents and interests. The wife of a seminary professor and the dean of the theology school encouraged me to pursue doctoral work. I firmly believe that few people receive a clearly defined call from God. God speaks to them gradually through other people and through circumstances."

Part of the call experience is the recognition by women seminarians that they have the kinds of gifts that would make them effective leaders in a church setting. These gifts fall into various categories. Some are related to the area of administration. Seminarians spoke of their organizational ability, their creative response to problem situations, their ability to identify the crux of a matter quickly and to act decisively. Others mentioned that they enjoy interacting with people and are able to delegate effectively and to include others in decision-making processes. An outgoing personality, self-confidence, assertiveness, and broad perspectives combined with a deep love for people and a desire to serve are qualities widespread among the seminarians questioned. Many were aware that they have good verbal skills and are able to communicate theological ideas effectively. A talent for public speaking made the preaching and teaching aspects of pastoral work attractive to these seminarians. Some mentioned that they are good listeners, able to empathize with others and to identify with their hurts and joys. Patience, optimism, and the ability to take criticism were also considered to be aptitudes that would enable a person to function well in a leadership role. When they are able to put these aptitudes to work within the context of the local church, women seminarians have found that they achieve an inner peace and a sense of fulfillment which creates within them a growing awareness that they are called to ministry.

For all of this, there are among the ranks of women seminarians some who are wondering whether in fact they will ever be able to use their gifts, knowledge, and expertise within their own denomination. One student wrote, "So here I am—soon with an M.Div. and some parish experience—waiting, praying that God won't take too long to convince the males that I'm gifted and called by the same Creator who designed them." Another spoke of her call to priesthood as "a prophetic calling for a woman in my Catholic tradition." A second-year student from Louisville Presbyterian Theological Seminary found it necessary to change her denomination in order to fulfill her call: "My home church is a new one; I changed from Baptist to Presbyterian just this year because of the openness to women in the Presbyterian church." Another respondent chose to stay within her denomination even though she found herself beset by problems: "Our Roman Catholic system is one I'm comfortable with, but it creates a tension in me because at times I don't accept the official party line."

Even those who feel strongly called to ministry are sometimes tempted to take a side-glance toward a career less fraught with tension. A second-year student at Gordon-Conwell Theological Seminary reflected, "I am also interested in college administration. People are more open to women in that field than they are to women in church leadership." Occasionally the stressful atmosphere proves too much and a woman seminarian will choose to enter another sphere of work: "I didn't have the personal strength to cope with the criticism I got from evangelical Christians. It is easier to pursue a career in the business world, which I am doing. I may minister a little 'on the side,' but basically I've been scared away from serious Christian work." It would be presumptuous to conclude that such a person was "never really called" to ministry. Rather, the church must accept with shame the responsibility for having discouraged from service one whom God had called and equipped.

The years of seminary training provide an opportunity to think and evaluate. Not every woman seminarian is 100 percent sure of her calling, but many feel a strong urgency about pursuing the matter of ordained ministry. A student at the Theological School, Drew University, expressed it this way: "God may not have tapped me on the shoulder to join the team, but I really feel this is 'my calling,' and I'll continue until an equally clear message to the contrary comes through."

Seminary Experience

Seminary faculty are influential people. They not only guide seminarians through academic studies, but they also provide role models in a variety of other spheres such as preaching, counseling, community involvement, and family relationships. It is to the faculty that seminarians look when they are seeking insight into the complicated issues relating to church leadership. Many of the seminarians who responded to questionnaires spoke very positively of the faculty with whom they had studied. They reported that a number of professors in their respective schools had affirmed them as women and as potential ministerial candidates, that their opinions were respected in the classroom, and that for the most part they found their teachers to be understanding, helpful, and encouraging. However, some students reflected sadly that they had little contact with faculty and that they were forced to seek affirmation and advice elsewhere.

Why do some women feel a lack of personal involvement with the teaching structure of their school? A possible reason may be that seminary faculty are often heavily loaded with teaching and research commitments and simply do not have the time to spend with individual students, whether these students are male or female. But this was not often perceived to be the case by the seminarians themselves.

Sometimes the faculty's lack of interest was interpreted by the student as reflecting a judgment concerning the student's ability: "They always work with the obviously gifted . . . therefore, they've never noticed me because I'm another 'just average' student." Sometimes a seminarian sensed that faculty members, though well-meaning, seemed uneasy in coping with the situation of women in theological training: "The seminary welcomes us, but doesn't quite know what to do with us." "Some people, including professors, don't know how to relate to women in new roles." In order to compensate, certain faculty members adopt a paternalistic attitude toward women students—a stance that is much resented.

Some are patronizing: "Overly nice, but not seeing us as intellectual and creative equals." Others simply ignore women students: "It is humiliating never to be called on in class to pray. Some don't recognize us when we raise our hand to ask a question."

Being ignored is only one part of the story. Experiencing a negative attitude in the classroom is another. A large number of seminarians commented that such negative attitudes were often communicated by inappropriate jokes. "One professor has a very negative attitude toward women in ordained ministry, and to women in general. Some of his jokes in class have put women down. . . . We spoke to the academic dean, and things have improved." "The jokes get irritating and reflect what I believe is a lack of genuine understanding on the part of many of the males." Women feel at times that they are being "put down" unfairly: "On one occasion I heard a professor say that some women seek ordination because it is an ego trip for them. I spoke up and said, 'Why is it that the same question cannot be asked of men?' The professor dismissed the class without responding to my question." Some respondents complained of the tacit assumption that the women students in classes are either the wives of ministers or are preparing for the mission field. One student felt that inadequate reasons were given to account for the number of women entering seminary: "Some have said that the reason women are encouraged to come to seminary is that not enough men heed the call for them to come! My response has been that hopefully seminaries encourage women because they have something vital to contribute to the ministry."

A quite widespread phenomenon was the exclusion of women and their concerns from class content and presentation. One seminarian commented: "If professors would expand their views of ministry to include women, it would help. Not just tack on a comment at the end of a lecture." Many complained that noninclusive language was used persistently by instructors in spite of requests to the contrary: "Some professors use all male terms in lectures, and when they give examples they use male subjects. It is discouraging and causes one to feel left out." Criticism was also made of visiting professors who displayed crude attitudes and showed a lack of sensitivity to the issues. It was stated frequently that church history courses by-passed the contribution made by women and concentrated only on male personages as though they alone had contributed meaningfully to the history of the church.

It was felt by some seminarians that more discretion should be used in the selection of textbooks. One school uses a textbook on preaching which assumes throughout that the preacher is a man. It discusses how "he" should dress, stand, speak, etc. The text was published in the 1970s! Instructors, too, can make the same mistakes: "Sometimes in pastoral counseling the professor will start talking about how it is bad news to counsel a woman when there is no one else in the church building, or about how women sometimes fall in love with their counselors. There is not much commensurate time on how women counselors deal with the special problems of male clients." This seminarian commented, "The best thing I know to do in a situation like that is to talk with the professor." Another seminarian reported that instructors may sometimes allow unconscious prejudices to influence their grading system. "My husband gets higher grades in classes he takes with me. Some are deserved—some are not. Several professors have problems giving me a higher grade." A professor who changed his examination policy from named papers to social-security-number identification found that women scored much higher on essay questions than when names were used.

Some seminarians felt that the seminary curricula neglected broad areas of concern to women. When it came to exploring feminist theology, for example, some women seminarians found that they had to seek this out for themselves. Many suggested that seminaries should inaugurate courses on women's issues as part of the core program for men and women. These courses would encompass such matters as the place of married couples in ministerial settings; the particular challenges faced by single women in ministry; celibacy as a positive asset in church leadership; preaching and mental health; handling personal conflict; the menstrual cycle and its effect on professional performance; and the years of child-raising as a background to ministerial function.

Perhaps the most frequent complaint of seminarians was the lack of women faculty: "We are surrounded by male faculty members all the time." It was felt that having women professors would be an affirmation of the scriptural authority women have as teachers. Some respondents sounded quite desperate over this issue: "If we can't get a full-time woman on faculty, it would help to have an inter-term course with a woman . . . we don't see ordained women in a way we can get to know them and discuss issues. It would be good for the men to see a positive woman model." "They say they have tried in the last three positions they've filled—but I wonder. It's desperately needed." All were agreed, however, that only fully qualified women should be appointed and that they should be appointed to mainline positions, not merely to peripheral concerns and supportive services. It was clear that this desire was in no way to be interpreted as a criticism of the male faculty: "I have had classroom experience of ten or a dozen terrific male professors over the past two years." It was simply a matter of acquiring balance and providing a dimension of the educational experience that no male, however gifted, could provide.

The percentage of women faculty members in the schools represented was found to be incredibly low. The ratio of male to female faculty reads something like this: 30-0, 20-1, 34-6, 65-4, 46-0, 40-2, 21-3, etc. Unfortunately, it is rare to find the women faculty members in central teaching positions, such as theology. They are usually in positions such as counseling, Christian education, and music. This situation gave rise to such comments as: "Our one woman faculty member teaches Christian education. I strongly desire to see a woman with a theological background on the faculty. I do not know any woman personally whom I respect for her scholarship."

Apparently seminarians are informed that the reason for this lack is that as yet few women are academically qualified for these positions. While acknowledging that this may be true, seminarians still felt that women are not being given the prominence they deserve. Many suggested that women should be invited more frequently to preach in chapel or that qualified women should be hired to visit on campus for short-term lecture series: "Cynthia Jarvis, who is a professor at McCormick Seminary in Chicago, preached at our seminary for a week. It was a *great* experience." Some felt that resistance to this came from the administrators of their schools, and they suggested that schools should hire administrative personnel who are sympathetic to the cause of women.

Attitudes expressed by faculty naturally influence the male seminarians. One woman commented, "My first semester I was informed that women had a role in the church as teachers but not in leadership positions. When a seminary professor projects such a bias, how can one expect male students to feel different?" In fact, some male students arrive in seminary with a strong bias against women, and these occasionally make life difficult for women seminarians: "Sexism of male students is a greater problem than sexism of professors." Occasionally male students take it upon themselves to "caution" their female counterparts: "I've been taken aside to discuss the scriptural basis of my being here." Sometimes the men feel threatened by the high academic performance of women seminarians: "I know that my language abilities have threatened some guys who struggle with languages, and I'm sorry they feel that way." Ironically, the social and personal pressures women experience in seminary often drive them to greater endeavors in academic studies: "Many male students seem to feel a woman should be docile and submissive. As a result, I tend to excel academically but am hesitant to function on a spiritual or personal level." Sometimes women themselves encourage the development of hostile attitudes by the way they present their cause: "We have a problem with rather 'militant' female seminarians who are out to claim their 'right' to preach and exercise authority. . . . Women who try to claim the pastorate as a vocation by rights rather than as a calling of God make things difficult for the whole issue of women at seminary."

Such biases were also seen in social attitudes. Women seminarians often mentioned that while on the one hand it is assumed that a woman in seminary is there because she wants to marry a minister, on the other hand male seminarians are reluctant to date a woman whose career goals are similar to their own. In career guidance, some women felt that they are being encouraged into the types of positions which will "fill in" between seminary and marriage, on the assumption that marriage will terminate their careers, while men are treated as though they are seeking lifelong vocations. Women also found that when they do contemplate marriage, it is assumed that they will lower their academic goals: "The spring of my first year I became engaged to a fellow junior. We married that summer. I heard later that there were some men in school who believed I would change my program to an M.R.E. . . . they were wrong. I think they were responding out of their own insecurities and from their inability to conceive of a marriage in which both partners could ably and happily serve the church in an ordained capacity."

A quick look at seminary catalogs revealed that men and women are still featured in sex-stereotyped roles. For example, a photograph in the catalog from one very progressive seminary shows a group of male students hunched over books in the library. Above them are several life-sized portraits of men who were probably past presidents of the school. Another photograph features three women; they are sitting on the grass outside the library, talking. When a man and a woman are photographed together, the man is usually assuming the role of instructor. He is speaking (pleasantly and caringly) to the woman student, usually looking down at her from a podium. Such pictures communicate very clearly the hidden agenda behind the educational opportunities offered in any given seminary, and would-be seminarians might well take note.

Advice to Women Considering Seminary Training

In offering advice to incoming seminarians, respondents were realistic. Many recommended that the seminarian should search out a seminary supportive of women candidates so that studies might be undertaken in a healthy environment. The choice is not always an easy one. One seminarian wrote: "Consider carefully your seminary. If you choose a conservative one, you will face greater hurdles as a woman. If you choose one open to women, you may have to work out conservative theology on your own. You must evaluate which set of difficulties you would rather live with."

Because problems are bound to arise, the new seminarian is advised to maintain "a willingness to work through problems rather than to avoid them." In doing this, "acquaint yourself as well as possible with human nature." On the one hand, a woman seminarian should not be "defensive and easily offended"; on the other hand, she should be prepared to work to change those aspects of seminary life that stand in need of change. One respondent advised: "Work to get what you need. Talk with supportive male professors and develop seminars to deal with issues women face." Patience is needed if long-range goals of cooperation between men and women are to be realized: "Sometimes it takes time and caring and sharing to help break through people's preconceptions and prejudices, but the effort is usually mutually beneficial."

Advice offered frequently took the form of a caution. "Don't go in with a chip on your shoulder and view all men as chauvinistic." "Don't go into it [ministry] unless you feel the call and it stems from love. The church is not the place for you to grind your ax." "Seminary is not a place to find your faith, or a husband." "Women who are in seminary to prove a point help neither God nor women's rights." However, it was acknowledged that anger will arise from time to time and that it should be allowed to surface.

"Challenge the system prophetically—own rage and righteous anger as being necessary and important." A woman entering seminary must have "the ability to control and use her anger—I'm convinced it is an integral part of us, and perhaps our best hidden strength."

Overall motivation is an important factor with women seminarians: "I would advise them to have a goal to reach, a dream in which they see themselves living and working every day." "To survive in an almost male world you will need singleness of purpose and the assurance of God's support." Because of the wide gulf between "the dream" and "the seminary situation," an incoming seminarian should "learn to maintain a balance between idealism and reality. Loss of such will result in either bitterness or obliteration."

It was considered essential that a woman seminarian have a good self-image. An example came from one respondent: "I am confident, usually, and if I don't feel particularly confident, at least I dress well and speak clearly. I like people, and I think that shows. I can be organized. I feel I am approachable for criticism, new ideas, and friendship. I am always well-prepared." The new seminarian should be confident about herself and her role: "I feel that my attitude about my role greatly affects men's attitudes toward me—if I believe in myself, they do too." "Expectation," another seminarian wrote, "can be a self-fulfilling prophecy."

Because the seminary has traditionally been considered a man's world, there is a tendency for women to feel they must act like men in order to survive. Consequently many seminarians advised that new entrants should work to maintain their femininity at all costs. "Try not to be masculine in dress, approach, or style." "Be assertive without being aggressive." "Be gracious and earn respect carefully." The woman seminarian should "use the mind that God has given her to gently and reverently stand behind her call from God." Rather than measuring herself by her male peers, the woman seminarian is advised, "Keep your eyes on your own calling: realize you are unique and incomparable." She will need "wisdom and discernment as to what things should be ignored and what things should be politely but firmly addressed."

It is generally thought that women must be superior to men in order to achieve seminary goals. One commented, "Right now she has to be better than men at everything in order for people to accept her. I do not think this is a fair expectation, but it will pass in time." This, however, is not seen by some as too much of a deterrent: "A woman has to be better—a superior preacher, a good administrator, and a loving pastor. Unfortunately, with the current state of the ministry, no great effort is required for a woman to excel over the majority of clergy!" One respondent pointed out the dangers of encouraging only very capable women to enter seminary: "If only super-women dare seek the ministry, what of the common women God has more frequently called and gifted? Let's not be out to prove something."

By way of encouragement, new women seminarians are exhorted to "look straight in the eye, love, and never back down." It was suggested that they should express appreciation for the gradual changes which have come about for women and that they should build on these. In times of difficulty they should "remember that Christ, too, was not accepted as God's appointed one. He did not give up, but continued to proclaim."

Retrospect

The chapter which follows this one surveys the opinions of women who have graduated from seminary and are now actively involved in church leadership. In addition to the material covered there, these women provided significant reflection on their seminary experiences. They were asked if there were any ways in which the seminary of their choice might have done a more effective job in preparing them for ministry. Their responses fell into three categories. One group of ministers felt that seminary had prepared them well for their profession. A second group suggested improvements in seminary education in general, though not in particular for women seminarians. A third group gave recommendations for changes geared specifically to women students. (The schools these women had attended were diverse, and any overlap with the seminaries mentioned in the previous pages of this chapter was coincidental.)

The women ministers who felt that the seminary in which they had trained had done an excellent job in preparing them for professional work saw no areas where change is necessary. Their memories of the seminary experience were good: "I loved seminary, and I think that probably the best thing that happened to me was that I gained self-confidence and assurance about myself—this has served me well." "The faculty of my seminary were very supportive of the women and included women's issues as a matter of course." Some thought that one should not expect too much of a seminary education: "We can learn the theory of ministry, but the actuality of pastoring is practice and experience, and there can be no substitute for that." Some felt that the seminary should concentrate on academic training, giving a sound basis in all areas and leaving the student to apply this knowledge in the years of professional service: "The best preparation is the best academic training one can get . . . so that you have facility in all areas. The real world comes *after* that."

The second group of women ministers did acknowledge that there are areas of seminary education that need improvement, but these are not necessarily related exclusively to the preparation of women ministerial candidates. One commented: "Frankly, it isn't the women who need the special preparation half as much as it is the men who need to be exposed to the theology which includes women. It is the male ministers who have the problem." Some felt that not enough is being done in seminary to confront both men and women with the sex stereotypes that influence their thinking and acting: "More needs to be done in terms of putting both men and women in touch with the sexist stereotypes out of which they operate and the influence they have on all our lives." "The problem is that our classmates accepted us and cared for us, but when they left the institution, they took their own stereotypes with them." It was widely felt that in providing only male models the seminary is depriving both men and women of a healthy exposure to ministerial function. It was recommended that the cultivation of positive attitudes toward both male and female seminarians be encouraged: "It seems to me that simply fostering equality and acceptance is the best way to serve not only the women but the church as a whole. The attitude of male ministers is crucial to the welfare of women ministers. If men go through seminary seeing that women are just as competent, that will eventually foster more acceptance in the churches."

With regard to course content, some in this second group saw the present system of "options" as being a built-in weakness for the seminary. Even students intending to enter the pastoral ministry might, if they so desired, opt out of such basic courses as those in Christian education or preaching—even theology. One would assume that this is not the case in every seminary, but evidently it is in some. A desire was expressed that seminaries might better prepare candidates with respect to practical matters such as church administration and financial affairs. Some felt that spiritual leadership is not being effectively cultivated. For example, not only are seminarians sometimes inept at leading a group Bible study, but they are sometimes at a loss to understand how theology, worship, and "real life" connect and intertwine. They have not come to terms with their own experience of God and are therefore unable to communicate this effectively to others. "We learn a lot about theology and religion, but few of us have a clear sense of our own spirituality. We do not know how to talk about God, short of giving a testimonial about being 'saved.'"

Other areas in which these women ministers felt that seminaries would do well to strengthen their programs included human sexuality, group dynamics, and job placement. In the area of human sexuality, some would like to see "more direct dealing with sexuality issues and how these will affect ministry." It was recommended that more courses include sections on the psychology of men and women, in order to provide a base for mutually supportive relationships. Some felt that they had not been well-prepared to deal with the many aspects of human sexuality with which they were later confronted in their congregations. In group dynamics, a need was expressed for training both with respect to team ministry and to working cooperatively with a congregation. Some felt that the seminary fosters an attitude of separation between the congregation and the minister rather than identity: "I found that there was a tendency to refer to congregations as 'they' (vs. 'us'). We need to come to terms with the fact that real people make up a congregation, people who are hurting and who need pastors to care for them, to listen to them, to be present with them." In regard to job opportunities, some would like to see the seminary communicate "more sophisticated knowledge as to how the placement system works, and especially concerning how to use 'informal' helps." This would include an honest assessment of financial remuneration to be expected: "Seminaries need to help all students see the realities of life in the parish, including the competition for parishes that pay a living wage. As a student, I often found seniors disillusioned by the salaries they were offered. They need to know the realities all along."

The third group of women ministers felt that there are ways in which seminaries might better focus attention on the specific needs of women. It was suggested that more opportunities should be granted to women in the wider aspects of seminary life, including chairing of committees, development of publications, and involvement at all levels of decision-making. Not only would this give women much-needed experience in areas from which they may previously have found themselves excluded, but it would also "enable more of our male colleagues to be able to deal with us in constructive ways once we are out of the seminary." Some longed for the day when women seminarians would be given equal opportunities for field work. As a means to this end, it was suggested that seminaries should take a tougher line over this issue and that they should "refuse to send interns, pulpit supply, youth workers, etc., to any congregation which refuses women candidates for these posts."

Conferences and causes dealing with women's issues were highly recommended. One respondent wrote, "U.C.C. clergywomen recently held a national gathering at which they considered the uniqueness of their ministry because of their gender. Such meetings are helpful." Another respondent suggested that it is sometimes possible to integrate into the curriculum a full-length course dealing with women's concerns: "Three of us ordained women taught a semester course on *Women in Professional Ministries*. Sixteen women said it was very helpful. We tried to cover all the areas not covered in the standard curriculum . . . areas we wished had been covered when we were in seminary." In ways such as this it is possible to address specific problems that women will face and to provide some techniques for dealing with these.

There is a tendency for some women to feel inadequate in the areas of administration that concern finances and the upkeep of church property and equipment. The reasons for this are obvious. Society has tended to protect women from such areas of concern, and they have not been exposed to these in the same way that male seminarians have in their upbringing. One woman wrote, "The area of administration seems to be a problem for some of my friends as well as for me. We have a hard time believing we have the power we actually have and acting on it. A course in administration designed specifically for women would be good." Some felt that women should try harder to equip themselves in the more technical fields so that they would have more competence in the general running of a church.

Training in homiletics and counseling should also take into consideration the special problems women may face. Women would benefit from voice training classes: "High-pitched, un-trained voices are unpopular no matter how dynamic the woman is otherwise." Opportunities to develop specific gifts as a woman would be appreciated: "It would have been good for me to know that as a woman I might have a different technique of counseling from that of men." Women also need to be given latitude to develop a homiletic style that is not based on male models but is their own.

Many women had found that all too soon in their ministry they encountered various forms of opposition, and there were times when this opposition was the direct result of their being female. They felt that the seminary would be doing a good pre-paratory job if it would give some guidance to women in "how to sort out the 'flack' that occasionally comes. Is it directed to me personally, to women in general, or to women ministers in par-ticular?" And if there is any way in which seminaries could help women cultivate the ability to "turn away a put-down with a smile and without inward wounds to self-esteem," then it would cer-tainly be valuable to attempt this. In these ways the woman semi-narian would be prepared for the "discrimination and pain within the parish" with which she will probably meet: "To me, knowl-edge is a way to conquer fears, and being forewarned makes any struggle more constructive in the long run." "Being prepared or 'aware' helps us not to personalize too much." The seminary is doing a fine job if it can enable women seminarians to achieve "self-understanding, so that we do not become easily threatened or overly aggressive." And when opposition does come, the woman minister is going to need a supportive community around her. Seminaries could help "by encouraging women to be an intentional support network with one another. Many of us did not perceive the value of this till we had gotten out 'on our own.' Any woman who thinks she can make it without the sisters' support is fooling her-self."

It was suggested that seminaries could definitely improve in the area of developing realistic expectations for the future. "Tell women the truth—that they will have to work hard for acceptance, twice as hard as men," one respondent recommended. Seminaries should also "quit encouraging women that the church in the world is ready and waiting for their talent and abilities": "Young women seem to be naïvely unprepared for the fact that by and large the churches do not want women ministers, and it will be a long time before they do." Looking ahead to the time when seminarians assume parish responsibilities, the seminary might well attempt to "make them aware of the difficulties of communicating with people who are set in their ways and unwilling to accept them as leaders, let alone as pastors." The gulf between seminary life and the realities of the parish was sometimes found to be frighteningly wide: "Somehow impress upon us that seminary is radically different from the world of ministry. Inclusive language, creative worship, equal opportunity for work, which are, in my experience, more the 'norm' in divinity school are unknown or infrequently realized elsewhere." One minister wrote, "I feel like I was so sheltered in a feminist cocoon that I was unprepared to serve a congregation with no raised consciousness at all—or any desire for such." And another commented, "It's a bitter blow to face the world equipped and encouraged, only to be shattered by the cold, hard facts of unacceptance as a minister."

The suggestion was made that seminaries might consider preparing students for small-church ministry in isolated settings in addition to the present emphasis on "steeple churches." Many women find themselves in small churches, and they need to be alerted to the special challenges of such ministry.

Finally, it was widely recommended that in view of the present shortage of female professors, ordained and experienced women clergy should be brought onto the campus on a regular basis for formal and informal meetings with women students. It was felt that this would enrich the seminary experience immensely. Women ministers also recommended that seminary professors should encourage academically gifted women seminarians to pursue careers in teaching, so that in the future the imbalance in this area might be redressed.

Notes

[1]Students from the following institutions participated in this project: Asbury Theological Seminary; Bethel Theological Seminary; Columbia Theological Seminary; The Theological School, Drew University; Duke Divinity School; Fuller Theological Seminary; Gordon-Conwell Theological Seminary; Jesuit School of Theology at Berkeley; Louisville Presbyterian Theological Seminary; Midwestern Baptist Theological Seminary; Pacific School of Religion; Southeastern Baptist Theological Seminary; Southern Baptist Theological Seminary, Louisville; and Trinity Evangelical Divinity School. The questionnaire used is printed in Appendix A.

WOMEN
IN MINISTRY

ONCE SEMINARY DAYS are left behind, the woman minister faces many challenges as she begins her professional career. If she chooses to enter the pastorate, as many women do, she may encounter initial problems in finding a church that she feels is suited to her leadership potential. This will depend to some extent on her denominational allegiance. In some denominations the local church has little to say in the choice of a minister; the decision is made at the state or national level. In other denominations the local church is autonomous. Such local churches may be far distant from the seminary in their stance on the leadership of women. Even after appointment to a pastorate, a woman minister must be prepared to face some problems which are directly related to the fact that she is a woman filling what has been for many centuries a male role. If change is slow in coming about in the seminary, it is even slower at the congregational level.

The substance of the material in the pages which follow was gained from direct contact with women ministers. Questionnaires were sent to women across the United States who are in some way involved in professional church leadership. Nine major Protestant denominations were in cluded in the survey.[1] In spite of heavy commitments and a proliferation of ques- tionnaires, many of these ministers responded enthu- siastically with detailed comments and even with letters of encouragement and support. Many took the time to recommend various books or denominational materials, listing sources from which these might be obtained. Although the sampling was necessarily selective, the completed questionnaires did provide direct insight into the situations faced by some women in church leadership positions.

Support and Placement

When a young man chooses to enter the ministry, he usually experiences the enthusiastic backing of his local church. Some women also found this to be true, but many discovered early in their commitment that such encouragement was not to be taken for granted: "I do remember that there was no glory or excitement about my commitment to the ministry such as there is when men make that decision." In practical matters, too, it was common to encounter quiet resistance: "By the church and the presbytery where I grew up, in a conservative area of South Carolina, I was ignored. My papers would be lost. I would not be contacted concerning meetings. I was never asked to preach until my final days of seminary—a different experience from that of male seminary students from my home church." When it came to ordination, some found similar problems: "My local 'district' refused to ordain me when the congregation requested this step. However, the Mennonite church has a congregational polity, and the congregation appealed to the national leadership and chose to ordain me anyway." Such incidents cast a shadow over entrance to Christian ministry.

Most of the women questioned, however, reported very positive experiences, both in their home churches and in their initial placement into a pastoral situation. They had proceeded through the normal denominational channels, had been interviewed for positions, and had been well-received. Some had obtained positions through informal "contacts," or because they had been highly recommended by one of their former teachers. Others had been approached by pulpit committees and had been offered very satisfactory appointments. Some had responded to advertisements in denominational journals and, after successfully completing the interview process, were appointed to pastoral positions. Many reported that in the placement process they had not encountered any problems which could be ascribed to the fact that they were women. Some said their gender had actually been an advantage because the churches in which they were interested were desirous of appointing a woman to their staff.

Of those women who had experienced problems in this area, some felt that these were to be attributed to the placement system itself or to the fact that this is largely administered by male personnel, many of whom are not sympathetic to the needs of women ministers. This was found by some to be the case in the seminary situation: "During seminary I received no help from the placement office, even for summer jobs." "The president (now bishop) of the L.C.A. synod to which I previously belonged refused to even try to place his women candidates and sent us looking elsewhere in the second semester of our senior year at seminary." Rather than being encouraged by administrators, these pastoral candidates found themselves being influenced away from ministry: "Our denominational administrators were full of scare stories about how few openings were available in the ministry—the implication being that even then women would only be called if no men were available." Another wrote, "My field education supervisor once suggested that I might be happier as a wife and mother." And one candidate was advised, "Wait until you are in your forties . . . you'll be more accepted as a woman minister when you are older"!

Many respondents said they would like to see the placement of women promoted much more strongly by administrators. It was suggested that the techniques used by some actually mitigate against the interests of the woman candidate: "In the call process of my district, I seem to fall through every bureaucratic crack that opens. The problems seem to be: (1) congregations' lack of experience of a woman pastor and (2) the district's tentativeness in giving my name. For example, they will 'check out' a congregation's attitude instead of just giving my name where my qualifications match the needs of the congregation." Some felt that they were too much in the dark about the whole process: "Because of our Baptist polity, pastoral candidates do not know where their names are being circulated, so we don't know which churches will not consider us because of our gender." "The church operates politically by word of mouth . . . women are outside most of the circles of conversation." It is in denominations where this "unofficial" power structure is permitted to operate that much of the problem lies: "'No openings available,' I was told again and again."

It was generally thought that congregations are more willing to take a chance with an unknown male than with an unknown female. Few churches, however, are prepared to give that as a reason for not calling a woman as pastor: "Churches don't say they won't hire a woman. Other reasons for dissatisfaction are given." Often the reason a candidate is rejected can only be surmised: "I suspect that various congregations in the areas I listed as 'preferred' did not pursue further contact with me because of my being a woman." But because nothing has been directly stated, there can be no grounds for objection: "I have applied to several parishes for the position of rector, and I do not believe my applications were ever seriously considered because of my being a woman. But I have no proof of that." Subtle methods are sometimes used to discourage a woman candidate from even applying for a position: "One committee described their situation as very bleak and uninteresting. I visited it later and found it quite appealing." Because of the reluctance of some churches to entertain the thought of a woman minister, it is often hard for a woman to obtain a hearing: "Some churches feel that it would be detrimental to their image to hire a woman. My biggest problem was calming fears and obtaining a chance to be heard."

Being highly qualified is not always the solution for a woman desiring to enter professional ministry. One candidate reported that although her qualifications were rated higher than those of her male competitors, "questions would arise relating to 'whether they could handle a woman pastor.'" Many women noted that there were times when they received no reply after applying for jobs for which they were fully qualified. Leaving seminary is a critical time, and a time at which it is easy to make comparisons of one sort or another. A respondent wrote, "I was the last person in my seminary class to receive a call upon graduation, in spite of the fact that academically and in terms of ministerial ability I ranked at the top." When applying for jobs, some women were actually told they were overqualified: "I found it very difficult to find work in Nashville, Tennessee, when I came here in 1978. It seemed that I was overeducated." Observing the struggle which some competent women have in finding employment causes other to question how much support they really have in the church structure: "One other woman clergy in this presbytery has interviewed for several positions and has not been called to any. She is one of the most competent people I know. So I do wonder about the real support of women clergy."

Anger was expressed by some women regarding offensive interview questions and comments. One respondent stated, "Two single women clergy I know were asked directly at job interviews whether they were lesbians. Are men asked if they are homosexuals?" Another wrote, "I was told by one church committee, headed by a woman my age, that I would not be able to appreciate their large eighteenth-century parsonage because I did not have a family." Others were asked if they contemplated marriage in the near future, and married women were interrogated concerning the number of children they expected to bear!

Anger was expressed by others concerning the fact that women are often relegated to "leftover" parishes with very low salaries and little hope of promotion. "I am angry" wrote one, "that many of us are forced to take jobs in small parishes which a 'real pastor' doesn't want; that there is pressure to fit that mold."

"The churches that are interested in women usually feel they could not attract a man for the salary or challenge they have to offer," observed another writer. Highly qualified women come out of seminary only to find that their options are severely limited: "The real problem is the narrow range of positions open to me. Small, rural, multi-church field, or associate pastorships. I want more options than that." "Most 'good' churches are not open to me, and probably never will be." One respondent observed, "No women in my denomination are serving parishes of over 150 members; only a few are serving parishes of over 75 members." If a woman wishes to obtain a senior pastorate, rarely can she find that in a large church: "If I had waited for a church senior pastorate, it would have had to be in a small church with a low salary." This was found to be particularly true in the South.

A woman whose husband is also an ordained minister will probably find it easier to obtain employment, although this situation does present its own special problems. "Our parish has admitted to its liberal and open-minded self that it would not have hired a woman pastor had I not come equipped with a husband who was also ordained." The obvious problem is for both to find employment in the same general geographical area. Occasionally both pastor in the same church. If the church is large enough, both work full-time; otherwise, each pastors part-time. Reports were that the part-time arrangement was very satisfactory when the couple was also raising a family because child-care could be shared equally between husband and wife. Sometimes two different churches were pastored by the clergy couple, and occasionally the wife worked within one denominational structure and the husband in another. One couple, for example, pastored respectively for a United Methodist church and a Lutheran Church in America congregation. This was the only way "to find suitable options for both of us." When it is time to move to another appointment, some couples have this equitable arrangement: "My husband and I take turns in job choices. This move he got first priority."

Problems other than geographical location can arise. Role stereotypes, for example, may cause trouble. One couple met up with a presbytery executive who was "convinced that clergy couples could work only as associates at a large church, the woman in Christian Education of course." Sometimes couples encounter authorities who feel that "any couple in which the woman is more verbal, assertive, or skilled than the man . . . or even equally so . . . is unbalanced and therefore unacceptable"! Occasionally the man may lose a position because he wishes to work in partnership with his wife: "My husband and I applied for a four-point charge and were turned down because they did not want a woman on the team of four." One woman who had lost her spouse feared that she might have difficulty finding a suitable appointment in the future: "I expect now to have some trouble in making my next move, since I am seeking a senior pastorate on my own."

Problem Areas

Once a woman is appointed as pastor of a church, she may find that she is the victim of all kinds of prejudices. One woman found that there was divided opinion in her church concerning whether or not she should participate in the preaching ministry: "In my first position there was concern about me preaching. I worked out an agreement whereby I would preach twice and then we would evaluate. The response from the congregation was so favorable that there was no problem." Another encountered opposition over the celebration of the eucharist: "I went to celebrate communion once in a congregation I served and where I regularly preached. They had taken the communion vessels away from the building. I addressed the congregation briefly on the subject and returned the next Sunday . . . they had everything prepared. All but one received communion."

The conducting of baptisms, weddings, and funerals is sometimes a problem area. A respondent wrote, "I was assistant pastor in a congregation of one thousand members. I was never asked to do a baptism; I conducted only a few funerals and no weddings. A large part of the problem was a senior pastor who was unwilling to share this aspect of ministry and so controlled the situation." This experience was by no means uncommon. One minister commented, "It seems to me that this type of problem is often due to an insecure or egotistical senior pastor." At other times it is the wishes of the congregation which predominate: "Some people still want a male minister for funerals—why, I don't know. Weddings are different. I've had no problems here." Non-church members who wish to be married in a church are apparently more likely to be conservative in this area: "We do a lot of non-member weddings, and then the request is for a male pastor." Performing a wedding in another diocese may also create a problem: "I was not allowed to perform a wedding in another diocese for two of our students. The bishop forbade it."

Pastors who are single experience some pressures not shared by their married colleagues. They do not have the ready-made support structure that may be found within a family unit—and there is no one to care for their needs when the day's work is over. Many of the concerns of church life cannot be voiced indiscriminately among a wide group of people, and a sense of isolation may readily develop unless there is a close support person in whom to confide. It takes effort and discipline to overcome this problem, and often the demands of church involvement drain away the energy needed to build a support network. Dating is another problem: "How many men are ready to date their pastor? Believe me, not many!"

However, those women who are already married when they enter the pastorate feel that they, too, have problems. One respondent wrote, "My guess is that the Protestant Reformation really hasn't gone much past the concept of married priests." She had in mind the care of children and the constant pull to be "both mother and pastor." Ironically, our society has reconciled itself to the male version of the dedicated pastor who is so involved with the family of God that he neglects his own family. It is assumed that his spouse will make up for the loss by being both father and mother to their children, even though she herself might be feeling neglected. The male minister is not only excused for allowing this situation to develop—he may actually experience a certain quiet approbation. But when it comes to the female version of the dedicated pastor, society's expectations are different. And because she is a product of this society, a woman's sense of responsibility is sometimes stronger in this area. A minister who is also a mother must constantly evaluate the quality of service she is giving to the church and the quality of nurture and support she is giving to her own family. Many women ministers consider themselves fortunate to have husbands who share equally in the task of child care. Potentially this situation can make ministry even more meaningful: "Part of being a woman involves the possibility of husband and children. My ministry has been enriched by these experiences." There are times, however, when serious choices must be made, whether or not they are understood by others: "I was three weeks pregnant when the accident at Three Mile Island occurred. To escape from the risk of nuclear contamination, I resigned . . . the lack of support and help is more than I can deal with here."

Women ministers were asked whether there is any appreciable difference between the salaries they are paid and those paid to men in similar positions. Some replied that they are paid on the same scale as men and that they have no complaints in this area: "Since E.R.A. was passed in Pennsylvania in the late 1960s, I have had equal pay." Others said that they receive higher salaries than those paid to men in their positions: "Our synod is, if anything, fanatic in the opposite direction." But some stated that their salaries are "painfully different" and that "promotion" or "financial growth" is nearly impossible. Sometimes the reasons given were that the size of the parish precludes larger payment or that the geographical area to which they were assigned is less wealthy: "Compared to my classmates, I would say probably $3,000 behind, partly due to geographical difference." There is not always an obvious reason for the difference: "Less qualified men in my graduating class received calls paying almost twice what I am paid," wrote one respondent. Another commented, "My salary is $2,000 to $4,000 lower than men in comparable churches." A third wrote, "I am $500 lower than most of my male counterparts." Even when serving in the same church as a peer, differences were discernible: "The work was . . . equally divided, but he received one-third more. He also had far more use of the part-time secretary."

When the matter of payment is raised in committee discussions prior to an appointment, women are frequently treated differently from their male counterparts. "Discussions with the call committee . . . on salary were centered on how much I 'needed' rather than the worth of the position," one minister commented. Another wrote, "I started at a lower salary than the other associate minister. The reason given—he was engaged to be married!" It is quite common for ministerial candidates to be told, "Single women do not need as much as married men." One respondent wrote, "Being single, I am supposed to be cheaper. Actually my colleagues' wives are the major wage earners in their homes." Others commented that being single not only precludes a second income but also entails extra expenses, such as the need for a housekeeper. This was felt to be most unfair discrimination. Some women speak up actively and attempt to bring about change: "I am earning more than my predecessor simply because I told the committee that I deserved more than they were offering me."

Housing allowances are also an issue when discussing salary. One woman wrote, "I was the fifth woman to be ordained into this synod and the first to receive equal pay and housing allowance with the male graduates." A married candidate had this experience: "The Board of Trustees saw no need to provide a housing allowance because 'your husband does that.' When I suggested that they could give me a matching sum as part of my salary, they did offer $2,000 as a housing allowance. In the Chicago area where I reside, $10,000 is recommended." Clergy couples also face problems in this area: "As a clergy couple, my husband and I have encountered many people who assume we would be 'two for the price of one.' We both work full-time and expect to be paid accordingly." Some clergy couples take for granted that they will receive less than their due: "My husband and I are slightly underpaid since we share housing, thus relieving each parish of half of its housing cost. This is because we are a clergy couple."

Pressures resulting from prejudice are not always easy to isolate. Some feel that to find acceptance it seems to be necessary to repress the feminine side of their natures, and they offer strong resistance to this. "Many women, myself included, feel the pressure to fit in as 'one of the boys,' to abandon the feminine/womanly sides of ourselves in order to fit the clergy role," wrote one minister. "The image of the minister is male. That's a tough mind-set to break."[2] Some have a hard time combating feelings of inferiority: "We have been brought up to feel inferior to men." For others, coping with anger is a problem: "I think women's biggest problem is their anger which, though very real and honest, prevents them from going on with life and ministering effectively." Some feel they constantly represent not just themselves but all women, so that if they fail in any area they are somehow vicariously causing all women to fail. In this connection, many women are tired of being treated as "zoo exhibits" representatives of the species rather than individual people with dreams and feelings. As ministers of churches, women find themselves "visible walking targets for the pain, confusion, and grief that people feel over the changing roles of women and men in society at large."

Some women ministers said that they understand why some congregations are slow in accommodating to new forms of leadership. "It is never easy for people set in their ways to change, and the people who are most faithful to the church are many times looking for stability in the midst of a chaotic world. They don't want to have to deal with change in their religion, too. This is especially so when the pastor has been a strong father figure and has helped them weather the struggle." So congregations also have problems. On the positive side, however, it is good to be reminded that "the entry of women into the ordained ministry is not primarily a problem to be solved, but a gift to be received and appreciated and enjoyed." Perhaps this is the aspect which should be stressed.

Relationships

By virtue of her office a woman minister is committed to the establishment of a network of relationships. First she must establish rapport with ministerial colleagues within her church, and then with those ministers of other denominations who serve churches in the same general community. If she is fortunate enough to have a secretary and other staff members, she must aim to develop a working relationship which is mutually helpful. Her relationships with the church congregation are highly significant, as are those with the community beyond the church boundaries. While many women ministers have found few problems in these areas, some have encountered situations which have, from time to time, hampered their ministry.

Many women find themselves working as associate ministers where the other members of the ministerial team are male. Relationships in this situation are, as one respondent noted, "a real challenge and a real chance for all of us to grow." Another respondent wrote, "The biggest hassle will come from colleagues, and the more successful you are the worse it will be." Another reported she was having "much difficulty" in this area but was "not sure how to understand it." Below the surface of church leadership activity, women ministers commonly experience "subtle sexist attitudes that are hard to point out and difficult to deal with on an emotional level." This is often attributed to the fact that "pastors who come from male-dominated seminary days just do not know how to relate to a female colleague." The situation is one to which men have difficulty adjusting: "Some men have a hard time dealing with women as professional equals. I try to remember that it is their problem, not mine."

This underlying tension surfaces in a number of ways. A senior pastor may express his true feelings not in open hostility but in persistent betrayal of the working relationship: "The senior pastor I worked with was continually by-passing me and demeaning me." At other times paternalism is evidenced: "The underlying message is that women, and especially young women, are sort of defenseless and helpless and need someone to watch over them." This reveals itself in condescension: "They tend to be a bit condescending because they are not used to treating a woman as a peer—just check the way they treat their wives." A show of strength on the part of the woman minister is sometimes resented: "Strong women are expected in the ministry, but the first to complain about strength is the male pastor." When a task has been performed with excellence, casual comments may betray an attitude of disrespect: "I preached for a district ministers' retreat. Most of my male colleagues were supportive and complimenting; however, one told me later that he liked 'girl preachers' because they were prettier than men. . . . I did say that I did not consider a twenty-eight-year-old female a girl."

Women ministers may find that the only way a male colleague has been programed to relate to women is with sexual flirtation. Unhappily, this is common in the business world, and it is hardly surprising to find that it carries over into church life from time to time. Women ministers develop their own ways of dealing with this: "Occasionally a male colleague is patronizing, flirtatious, or rude. I try to use humor in confronting them." This places a restraint on the quality of friendship which can be developed: "It is difficult in many cases for me to maintain a warm and supportive relationship with certain colleagues without that warmth being taken as an invitation to a different kind of relationship." Pastors' wives, all too aware of the dangers, may discourage their husbands from establishing meaningful relationships with women colleagues:

"From what I have heard, I am a threat to many of the pastors' wives, and therefore, the coffee . . . and conversation are much harder to come by." When informal gatherings of male and female colleagues do materialize, the conversation is not always of mutual interest, and it may even cause alienation: "Male sexual humor gets to be a bore and a topic that separates us."

From time to time women ministers participate in clergy gatherings which include ministerial staff from other parishes or from other denominations. These gatherings, too, may present problems. The presence of a woman may be resented by certain people: "Some of the men in my area are tense when I'm at meetings. In my Baptist clergy group I find far less problem than in the ecumenical circle. It's nothing specific—a general feeling of avoidance or distance." Often at such gatherings the woman minister feels she is being ignored: "For the first year I was ignored by 75 percent of the other clergy in the district. Only after I confronted them with the distance and the hostility did a few of them acknowledge that they had 'difficulty in accepting me.' Now they at least say 'hello.'" Not every person has the emotional resources to effect an open confrontation: "Early in my ministry I quit attending most clergy gatherings because I didn't appreciate being treated like a sweet little girl instead of a colleague." One woman said she was referred to constantly at presbytery meetings as "the blonde"! Another reported that she faced derision and abuse: "At a clergy gathering I was cornered by a fellow pastor. He said, 'Am I ever thankful my wife isn't a pastor.' He was quite abusive." The president of one ministerial association insisted on addressing the group as "gentlemen," thus communicating clearly his attitude toward the woman minister. One respondent reported that a potential pastor in a clergy gathering "acknowledged my presence only when there was something he wanted me to do—his reason, 'I'm just a male chauvinist.'" Some women ministers make initial efforts to create good relationships within their districts but meet with only limited success: "When I began in my first parish, I invited six different area pastors to lunch or coffee, and only one, a Catholic priest, returned the invitation."

Establishing relationships within the wider community may also be difficult for a woman minister. One respondent observed: "My biggest problem is trying to become involved in the community. The most active service organizations in the community are exclusively fraternal organizations, and while I certainly qualify from a professional standpoint, I cannot be included because of my sex." Generally speaking, the Jaycees, the Lions Clubs, and the Rotary Clubs all exclude women members. Influential people in the community tend to gravitate toward these associations, and many male ministers make significant contacts at these gatherings. There are no women's groups which serve quite the same function.

Relationships within the church are also important. A good secretary is a valuable asset in any setting, but particularly in a church. Many respondents spoke highly of the secretarial services at their disposal and of individual secretaries who excel in their work and provide an effective backup to the church's ministry. Warm, supportive relationships often develop in this area: "Secretaries are a real gift, so I support their work with my friendship." Most women ministers said that their relationships with church secretaries are good. Some attributed this to the fact that they view their secretaries as people rather than as functionaries and that they feel free to demonstrate appreciation for their services. There is genuine mutual respect in most cases. When problems do arise, it is usually because of divided loyalties. Occasionally a senior pastor insists on calling the church secretary "my secretary." Under these circumstances the secretary is generally less eager to assist the woman pastor. A few women ministers unhappily find that they have "inherited" a secretary who is basically opposed to the concept of women in church leadership. Such a situation is fraught with problems.

In a team ministry setting, the relationship with the secretary may be more complex. Some women find that the secretary caters to the men: "The secretarial needs of my male colleagues are taken care of better and faster than mine." A secretary can readily project such attitudes to the congregation: "Our secretary tends to assume that people would prefer a male clergy person, and she refers calls to me only when the men are not around." One secretary made a point of communicating information to the senior pastor but not to the woman minister who was the associate. Small matters, perhaps, but collectively they can create tension and conflict: "The female secretary had great difficulty doing secretarial things for me, such as phone calls, letters, arranging appointments." Initial setbacks can sometimes be overcome: "This was an area of concern for our secretary before I came, but it has turned out to be a very positive relationship." Some women ministers have male secretaries, and they find this very satisfactory.

Relationships between a woman minister and her congregation are highly significant. Most of the respondents find their congregations warmly supportive of their ministry. One wrote enthusiastically: "I must really compliment my parish on their adventurous spirit and very open and relaxed attitudes." "Overall I've found overwhelming love and acceptance, if not excitement about my ministry as a woman." On rare occasions, negative attitudes have been encountered, but these are the exception. One writer responded: "Once in three years someone left the altar rail rather than have the chalice from me. Other than that, the congregational response has affirmed me as a priest tremendously." Another observed: "Very warm, affirming people in the churches I've served. Usually at first there are a few people who won't come or have preconceived notions about woman ministers, but these get handled individually or sometimes get cleared up spontaneously as time passes." The respondents felt that a woman minister's attitude is very important: "If a woman goes into a situation expecting problems because she is a woman, she will most likely be able to find them. If she goes in confident and open, she will overcome any initial reticence fairly quickly."

Even with the best of attitudes, however, a woman minister may expect to encounter some opposition. One respondent reported that a woman in her congregation "said that it made her physically ill to see and hear a woman in the pulpit"! Another commented, "I also work with youth, and I find that many of the mothers wanted a 'good-looking male' minister for their kids." Other women in the church may deliberately cause trouble: "Some of the women in the power structure of our church's women's auxiliary are very negative and even hostile. This is changing a little bit, but it will continue to be a difficult area." When opposition is voiced, it should be given a fair hearing: "We cannot deny that women in the ministry is new—our human nature is to find security in the old. It is important to respect and hear reluctance when it is voiced." At the same time, some felt that church leaders should not shy away from exposing attitudes that fall short of the Christian ideal. A need was expressed for "bishops willing to point out bigotry and discrimination for the ugly thing it is. We are often slow to point out to Christians how unChristian their behavior can be—till they no longer can see right from wrong."

Opposition is sometimes encountered from lay people who are very rigid in their attitudes and expectations. These occasionally find it hard to accept a woman as an authority figure, and they are surprised to find that a woman minister can actually operate effectively when conducting the business side of church affairs. One writer commented, "No matter how angry I've gotten, I have neither cried nor screamed at a church meeting, and I have been told that I am less easy to bully than most of my male predecessors." Attitudes are sometimes expressed in the way in which a lay person addresses the minister: "I could always tell how people felt about me by the way they addressed me: first name—friend; Ms. X—doubtful about my pastoral role; Pastor X—everything okay." There are lay people who cannot bring themselves to give a woman minister her correct title: "One of my elders introduced me to his mother as the preacher's wife even though my husband had never preached in that church!"

Physical appearance has a bearing on relationships with the congregation. For men entering church leadership positions physical attractiveness is usually considered a plus. A "young, good-looking" minister is to be coveted. Women do not find their youth and attractiveness valued to the same extent: "My age (26), being single and a rather attractive woman are three aspects that can cause some to be hesitant in trusting my capabilities," one respondent observed. Another bemoaned, "Physical attractiveness is both a blessing and a curse. It gets attention, but it's such a hassle dealing with people's amazement at a pretty woman being a minister ('You don't look like a minister!')." Why is it assumed that a beautiful woman would not enter professional church leadership? Why will a congregation adulate a handsome young male minister but be wary of an attractive young female minister? A pregnant woman minister may also have misgivings about the response of the congregation: "Now that I'm very pregnant and beginning my summer supply preaching, I wonder how congregations will react."

On the whole, congregational response was not seen to be a major problem, and positive attitudes were expressed: "Rely upon people to be fair in the long run . . . 98 percent of the congregation will be." When opposition was encountered, it usually proved to be temporary: "There were three families opposed to the woman pastor. In the first year of ministry they were all 'back in the fold.'" "The four who voted against calling a woman are now among my staunchest supporters." "A year later there are people who come up to me and say 'I didn't want you to come, but now I say "Why not?" and I'm glad you're here.'" The respondents felt that women should not react to opposition by downplaying the role of male members of the congregation but rather by enhancing it: "I fear that women, in their effort to succeed at their job, frequently discourage the participation of men in the congregation. That could be a serious mistake which will take a long time to rectify."

Congregations, it seems, have a fairly clear picture of what they expect in the way of leadership. A woman who is competent in fulfilling her duties is likely to be accepted and appreciated: "The Lutheran laity has an ingrown understanding of the office of the pastor, and when they see that a woman is fulfilling that function, they relax and everything is fine." Perhaps, after all, it is the function that is significant. The gender of the minister becomes a somewhat insignificant factor: "In this last year I think they've found that the differences between male and female pastors are really minimal." Congregations do readily adapt to changing situations, and they sometimes surprise themselves with their changing attitudes: "In all three congregations the process was about the same—Step One: 'I never heard such wild ideas. We have never done it that way.' Step Two: 'Things sure aren't dull any more. The young people are really taking an interest.' Step Three: 'Why do you think you are called somewhere else? We need you here just as much as any place else needs you.' Step Four: Somebody else takes over, and it all goes better than it would if I were there. Churches are filled with leadership."

Personal Issues

Women ministers struggle not only with interpersonal relationships but also with inner feelings. They are not immune to doubts, fears, and personal problems. There are times when doubts may be particularly strong: "Just as all ministers have doubts, so do I. The call is not always overpowering, and questions of my abilities and intentions frequently raise their ugly heads." A certain isolation accompanies this profession, and the single woman minister may have to grapple with such problems alone. Does she have the gifts needed for ministry? Is she effective in her professional performance? The tiredness that results from constant activity will often give rise to feelings of self-doubt: "My doubts have usually surfaced when I personally felt worn out by the constant demands of ministry." "When the work load is extra heavy or the problems in the parish cause frustration, I wish momentarily that I could get out. But then I find myself right back in again." It is not always easy to establish a good self-image, particularly early in professional life. Situations can sometimes prove to be quite devastating: "Rejection is one of the most difficult things for me to take, whether I'm a minister or not. But it is always lurking behind corners."

Alongside the usual concerns of church leadership, the woman minister is struggling with issues that relate to herself as a woman. Many of the respondents had heard very few women preachers during their seminary days, and many of them had not been fortunate enough to share friendships with other women ministers: "The first time I heard a woman minister preach was when I stood in the pulpit myself." "The first time I saw a female pastor in a robe was when I looked into my own mirror." Therefore, women from many denominations are independently questing after the significance of a woman's role in ministry: "I am constantly searching for answers to what it means to be a single female pastor." "I find myself struggling with what I specifically bring to ministry as a woman. The men I have spoken with see ministry more in terms of a neuter function. I cannot help but believe that, by being a woman, what I offer and how I offer it differs from the men I know in ministry." Sexuality must never be denied: "I am an attractive woman physically and very personable. I wonder often if the men in the congregation are responding to me as their pastor or as a woman. Probably both. I think so."

A woman minister must also grapple with fear and stress. Sometimes fear arises from practical situations: "Because I was not permitted to perform certain duties, I feared them. I do not now." "I experience fear when I start something new. Will I be seen as me, the person, or as representing all women Episcopal priests? I am not all women, only one." Sometimes the fears relate to intangible or imaginary situations: "I entertain fears of punishment for being both strong and female." "I feared that people might leave the church because I was a woman." In response to fear a woman minister will sometimes involve herself in frenzied activity, but this is self-defeating. Stress also results from "the need to appear strong and together when I am very aware at times that I am weak and apart." At times like these a woman minister may be conscious of her need of support: "Another problem is loneliness—for a woman friend or a mate who understands my fears and pressures." There are ways of dealing with this problem. "I joined several women's groups and am close friends with the local Roman Catholic sisters."

A woman minister must also deal with the issues of marriage and motherhood. "I think a married woman has a much easier time than a single woman," was a common observation. A single minister wrote: "I wish I could get over feeling that I have to be my wife as well as me." But when it comes to contemplating marriage, other considerations arise: "I wonder how I can marry and maintain my current 60–64-hour week at my career." One respondent observed. "I am a very domestic person. There were times when it seemed that ordination would prelude marriage and a family . . . and indeed it has not always been easy to combine them." The problems are not hypothetical: "My husband admits to some difficulties with my professional role, the limelight, the time commitment, etc."—an interesting reflection on cultural conditioning. Motherhood is another issue: "We are ready to start our family, and I have had some anxieties about the congregation's reactions. It's really none of their business, but that's easier to say than feel."

Personal problems there certainly are: "There seem to be more crucifixion than resurrection experiences. I don't know if I can sustain this." "Many times I have felt like Peter standing on the water with the waves rising and the wind howling." But women face these problems with courage and hope. Some work constructively to see that the next generation of women has an easier time: "I cannot sit back and let other women take the initiative in consciousness raising as I did when I lived in one area (Iowa) where there were many women pastors." Some find strength in the words of great church leaders of the past: "I was helped all the way through by a quotation from Martin Luther—'For progress is nothing other than constantly beginning. . . . We are always traveling, and must leave behind us what we know and possess, and seek for that which we do not yet know and possess.'"

Advice

Many women ministers were enthusiastic in recommending that other women pursue church-related vocations, "If you feel called and qualified, there is no better life." Many advantages were listed. Some felt that a career in church ministry fits in well with family life: "The variety is limitless. It is also a good vocation to combine with motherhood because even though demanding, you can juggle your time." This freedom to plan one's own schedule presented an attractive option to many, and the close involvement with people provides an opportunity for meaningful relationships to develop: "Working with people brings some of the greatest joy in life—and the greatest pain." It was generally felt that the joy outweighs the pain.

What advice would women ministers give to a seminarian about to assume pastoral responsibilities, and what qualities of character would they consider to be important? One respondent wrote, "I would share in her excitement, encourage her competency, warn her of possible cruelties and unfairness, and stand ready along the way to help her." Another would advise, "Don't consider it at all unless all other ways of serving God leave you with a feeling of desolation and disquietude." Some contributed very practical advice: "Marry someone whose career is movable." "Wait to begin your family until you're called to a parish." Others called for a realistic appraisal of the consequences of such a course of action: "Think about what it will mean to your personal life. Your whole life will be spent being a new idea—not so much a pioneer as a road-maker. People will admire, hate, envy . . . but if God wants you, it will work out."

As for qualities of character, the woman minister will require patience: "There has been real progress," but "it is going to take many years to overcome the bias and prejudice of centuries." She will also need persistence: "Perhaps tenacity is a better word—to keep holding on in the face of all kinds of odds." She will need considerable inner strength: "Can she handle the extra stress of having to prove herself over and over again?" Resilience is also needed. A woman minister must be able to "bend and spring back like a bamboo branch in stormy weather." The touchstone of her life must be "an obvious faith and devotion to God and to Jesus Christ"—this will give meaning to the struggle. The woman minister must be level-headed in a group situation: "In discussions she must be able to think clearly, express herself well, and not use inappropriate emotional responses or gambits." She must somehow achieve a balance between servanthood and assertiveness: "Do not let others intimidate you, but do not bulldoze over people in proving your rights." It will help if she has "the ability to listen and understand what the confusion or fear is behind the argument." At the same time she must cultivate the ability to say, "I can see what you are saying, but I want you to know that things like that do hurt me."

Self-image is very important: "It needs to be strong (yet not inflated) because there will be much in your future that will tear away at it." One pastor commented, "The women saints of history have troubled me. Following their models of humility and long-suffering has got me into professional hot water. A self-effacing style is NOT the most effective." A number of ministers suggested that women should take advantage of the abilities which have been developed as a result of their cultural conditioning: "We are taught to be nurturers, and that is a helpful role to develop." However, women should have the confidence to step aside from society's expectations if they feel their task demands such action: "People find it incomprehensible for a woman to put her calling above 'getting married.' If the two happen to be incompatible, only God really understands." Above all, women should develop their potential as women: "Don't be molded into a little man-minister."

The respondents also gave advice regarding training and goals. Flexibility is an important trait in this regard: "In my denomination, there are more clergy available than there are calls available. I would advise all prospective seminarians (both men and women) to prepare also for another profession in case they are unable to obtain a call." Some feel it is a mistake for either men or women to move directly from schooling to the pastorate: "I would advise not following the pipeline routine—straight from high school to college to seminary. Even a year of work experience is helpful between college and seminary." And it is considered wise to develop an open-minded stance in relation to denominational allegiance and to assess carefully where the individual may best fit: "Be willing to look at various denominations in which to work out that calling to the best of your ability." Many have found from personal experience that a change of denomination is beneficial: "I could not find a call within the L.C.A. for a year following seminary. . . . I accepted an appointment by the United Methodist bishop." "I was raised as an Episcopalian. When I looked for support from my church, I heard 'Go elsewhere.' I chose to become a Lutheran." "I moved from the Methodist Church to the United Church of Christ." "I moved from Catholicism to Lutheranism." Even given ideal conditions, women were cautioned not to imagine that they will necessarily be successful: "Not every woman who thinks she is called will be a success. Not every man is either." Women should be realistic about their abilities and should accept the fact that there is not room for everyone at the top: "Accept the truth that you may not get to Riverside Presbyterian Church in New York, but wherever you are called, God needs you there."

Concepts of Church Leadership

Women ministers were forthright in their opinions concerning the present concept of church leadership and the new directions they would like to encourage. Many felt that one of the biggest problems confronting the church is the fact that over the centuries the role of pastor has been viewed in terms of power rather than servanthood. Consequently, there has been a tendency for church leaders to grasp after status and to glory in their image as authority figures. This in turn has led to professional jealousy and to a competitive spirit which does nothing to enhance the gospel that the church proclaims. Respondents wrote, "The current stress on the pastor as authority figure cheats everybody and short-circuits the faith of many." "We talk about the priesthood of all believers, but too often the parish pastor ends up being the 'highest priest.' Leaders claim to be enablers, when what they are is manipulative and dishonest." "If the pastor begins by stepping down from the throne, then others can follow." It was felt that too often church people are encouraged to "turn a blind eye" to what is really going on in the administrative background of church life: "I think we are not very honest about 'power.'" "There is a lot of game-playing and politicking in the upper echelons that irritates me at times."

Many deplored the trend toward using business models as models for ministry: "These things don't match up." The present hierarchical structure of many denominations was felt to be cause for concern: "I think our hierarchical pattern is highly questionable." "Churches ought to move toward non-hierarchical patterns of leadership." Too often, it was felt, leadership is used "to distribute personal favors or reward friends," or even "to keep the lid on controversy." Congregations then become pawns in a system, often unaware of "what is really going on" behind the scenes. Manipulative methods are sometimes used to secure a "favorable" vote. It is assumed that "the minister knows what is best for the congregation," and the members of the congregation, like young children, are protected from acquaintance with the real issues and therefore from the possibility of using their own judgment and influence. Report sheets can conceal as well as reveal, and congregations eventually become accustomed to a vague feeling of uneasiness as church business is conducted with their apparent consent.

In some denominations this situation is changing. "More lay people are accepting their responsibility in decision-making, and more clergy are willing to loosen their grip on the reins of leadership." Many respondents felt that the key to this whole issue is greater involvement of the laity. It was felt that churches should aim to "revitalize the skills of the laity" and that the long-range plans of a church should be to so distribute leadership functions that a paid professional leader might become redundant, or at least might assume a very different role from that now assumed. Some deplored the fact that to a certain extent ministers are "paid to be the church": "My biggest frustration as a minister is not that I am a woman in a man's church, but that I am looked on as a hired Christian." "I'd like to see the need for a paid professional disappear." By what means might such an end be achieved? One suggestion was a return to the "small house church concept, with celebration as the body of Christ on Sunday mornings." Others recommended that the ministry skills of lay people should be developed and that they should be encouraged to minister to one another "in word and deed." It was strongly suggested that lay people should be featured more prominently in the leading of congregational worship: "I long for a worshiping, loving, serving community where everyone's gifts are welcomed." Too often the "paid professional" is expected to minister the full range of "spiritual gifts," when actually most of these are lying dormant within the congregation.

Are congregations realistic in their expectations of the leaders they appoint? Some respondents felt that far too much is expected of pastors: "Superhuman qualities are projected onto them. They cannot help but fall short of these. Then disillusionment sets in." Idealization is followed by devaluation, and there may be a feeling of discontent and disappointment. If congregations could accept their pastors as mere mortals, it would help: "We must educate the laity so that they see their ministers as persons. Sometimes laity do not realize that their pastors also feel grief, pain, disappointments."

Perhaps congregations assume that a professional minister needs more skills than one person can possibly combine. An interesting observation was made in relation to this: "I think we need some specialists. That is how doctors and other professions accomplish the best results." Another problem is the expectation that all ministers have the same leadership skills: "I think the biggest change is to realize that ministry and leadership come in many shapes and forms, and there must be room for a lot of variety."

The respondents commented, finally, on the need for outspoken prophetic leadership and for personal spirituality. A woman minister must come to terms with the true nature of her function: "My struggle is to find the creative balance between strong aggressive leadership and supportive, patient facilitation." Seminary training does not give all the answers; they must be sought: "I think at present our concept has done well with the enabling function but needs to also incorporate an assertive dimension. I think we're trained to listen well but not to actively take charge. Our church has reacted to the Herr Pastor image—but the gospel does need to be spoken. God not only listens but speaks. So, I believe, must God's ministers." "Our leadership needs to be more prophetic and less soothing. We need to take the risk and raise our voices." Some would like to see more emphasis on the role of the minister as an exponent of the biblical message: "I prefer a clear identification of the pastor as interpreter of God's Word which holds authority for all of life." This kind of spiritual leadership can come only from personal piety and careful study and it was felt that this should be encouraged: "I would like to see more emphasis on the minister as a spiritual leader, with time given for that spirituality to develop."

The search continues. . . .

Notes

[1]Responses were received from women ministers in the following denominations: "American Baptist; Christian Church (Disciples of Christ); Episcopal Church, Lutheran Church in America; Mennonite Churches; Presbyterian Church, U.S.; United Presbyterian Church, U.S.A.; United Church of Christ; and the United Methodist Church. Some denominations declined participation in the project and did not feel free to release the names and addresses of women ministers. The present situation in the Roman Catholic church explains the absence of respondents from this grouping. The questionnaire used is printed in Appendix B.

[2]See E. Margaret Howe, "Interpretations of Paul in the *Acts of Paul and Thecla*," *Pauline Studies*, eds. D. Hagner and M. Harris (Grand Rapids: Eerdmans, 1980), pp. 33–49.

MONEY
AND MINISTRY

ANALYSIS OF COMMENTS made by the women seminarians and ministers who responded to the questionnaires brought into focus an issue of more general dimensions than that of whether women should be ordained to ministry. The main concern of many of these women was not to seek out for themselves positions of honor equal to those of men. Rather it was a concern to establish a church leadership structure which would appropriately reflect Christian values and adequately serve the needs of Christians in community. In other words, women are not content merely to be appointed to the already existing structure. They are seeking to remodel that structure and to fashion it more in accordance with scriptural guidelines. In order to effect this, there has to be on the part of Christian people a willingness to rethink and if necessary to initiate change.

One area rarely addressed is that of financial remuneration for service given to the church. Earlier in this volume, reference was made to the fact that women have always played an active role in church leadership, but have not always been remunerated for this. There are other anomalies which could be cited which are not necessarily sexist, such as the fact that a church soloist may be paid for his or her performance while a Sunday school teacher may receive no payment. Are there scriptural guidelines which control this, and if not, on what basis are such decisions made?

Most churches employ men and women for ministerial service in a full-time capacity. There is much variation in the amount of money paid to a minister, and in some denominations the amount is dependent on the size of the church. Large, affluent churches will provide a salary comparable to that earned in other professions, and often higher than a person would earn in a secular educational setting given similar qualifications. In addition to the salary, numerous fringe benefits are enjoyed by the minister. These may include the provision of housing, car maintenance and running costs, conference allowances, and a variety of tax breaks. Often sizable sums of money are made available to enable an individual to pursue undergraduate or graduate studies. If the congregation served is small, or the geographical area is less wealthy, a minister may find that the salary offered is considerably less attractive.

Churches thus present a "market" for the ordained minister. A person who is appointed to a large urban church may be considered "highly successful," while a person serving a small agricultural community may be regarded as of lesser worth. In denominations that operate on such principles, "promotion" may be achieved through a network of "unofficial contacts"—personal recommendations often carrying much greater weight than objective indicators. Because of this, the minister may approach this profession much like the person who enters the business world, seeking to move from one financial achievement to another. As in the business world, the rules are not always clearly laid down. Aggressive, outgoing persons may "sell themselves" more effectively than certain of their peers. Solid achievement may be overlooked while sensational display is applauded.

In denominations where a more equitable system of financial remuneration for ministers is provided, "promotion" may be achieved in other ways. A hierarchy has developed in which state or national leadership carries greater honor and higher salaries than parish ministry. A person may for these reasons seek to move from the local to the state or national scene. Operating at the nerve center of denominational structure, a person will have access to funds which would be inaccessible at the lower levels of ministry. Such promotion may depend more on personal recommendations than on inherent worth or demonstrated achievement. For example, in the Roman Catholic church the decision-making process generally operates from the top of the hierarchy downward. Promotion may be conferred or withheld without any public accounting. The average member of a church congregation might prefer to quietly sidestep the issue of money and ministry. But downplaying an issue does not arrest unhealthy developments.

Biblical Guidelines

It is not known how Jesus and his first disciples financed their activities. Reportedly they traveled from place to place staying in the homes of friends or of those sympathetic to their message. Jewish custom did not permit a rabbi to accept money for teaching the Torah, the Jewish Law. Some Jewish rabbis, therefore, also practiced a profession or trade, and in this way supported themselves. One would assume that Jesus learned the trade of Joseph and was a carpenter. Several of his disciples were fishermen. That they did not abandon their trade is evident from the fact that they kept their boats and were able to return to them. If the public ministry of Jesus lasted for three years, as the fourth gospel indicates, it is very possible that Jesus traveled and taught on a seasonal basis, using the summer months for traveling and the winter months for work. However, the geographical extent of the ministry outlined in the Gospels is not large, and there is nothing in the account which precludes the possibility that Jesus and the inner circle of his followers undertook intermittent journeys throughout the year. Admittedly the argument is one from silence, but then so is the argument that they traveled and preached constantly during those three years.

As some of the disciples were already married, it seems reasonable that they would spend lengthy periods at home earning money for the support of their families. There were women, too, who traveled with the group, and according to Luke they "provided for them out of their means" (Luke 8:3). Unless one is to suppose that these women were independently wealthy, it must be assumed that regular earned income was available to them. Some of the women were probably wives of members of the Twelve, which makes it even more likely that these were working at a trade or profession at least intermittently during the public ministry of Jesus.

Although the Gospels are silent as to where the money came from, there certainly was money available for the use of the group. This money was apparently handled by one member on behalf of the others—Judas assumed this responsibility (John 12:6). When food was needed for the group, it was purchased with this money (John 4:8). It was evidently not a vast amount of money—certainly not enough to purchase bread at the cost of two hundred denarii (Mark 6:34-37). Giving money to the poor was a characteristic feature of Jewish piety; and, as a group of Jews, Jesus and his disciples certainly thought in these terms (Mark 14:5; John 12:4-5). Paul later stated as a principle of stewardship, that a Christian should endeavor to earn sufficient money to cover his or her own needs and the needs of others (Eph. 4:28). One may suppose that the early disciples were eager to exemplify this worthy aspect of Jewish commitment. Indeed, in his teaching Jesus took for granted that his disciples would involve themselves in such works of charity (Matt. 6:3). It is of interest, however, that when Jesus divided his followers into smaller groups and sent them into the villages to proclaim the coming of the kingdom of God, he explicitly instructed that they were to take no money at all with them: "Take no gold, nor silver, nor copper in your belts" (Matt. 10:9). Instead, they were to accept hospitality from the villagers if and when it was offered (Mark 6:8-10; Luke 10:4-7). On no account were they to accept money in return for their ministry: "You received without pay, give without pay" (Matt. 10:8).

There is thus no clear indication that either Jesus or his closest followers received financial support from others. The evidence suggests that they did accept hospitality from friends and sympathizers. At other times, food was purchased from a common fund. The fund was limited and probably necessitated the adoption of a simple lifestyle by the itinerant group. Why, then, has the church developed a tradition of a salaried professional ministry? If the Gospels suggest no such model, do the other New Testament writings provide a basis for this concept?

It is generally thought that Paul was one of the first "full-time" ministers. The church of Syrian Antioch commissioned him to travel in Cyprus, Asia Minor, and Greece, preaching the Christian faith and founding churches. Did this church finance his ministry? Apparently not. The only church from which it is known that Paul did accept money was the church at Philippi. When Paul wrote to thank this church, he stated, "It was kind of you to share my trouble" (Phil. 4:14). The opening section of the letter refers to the fact that Paul was in captivity: "You are all partakers with me of grace, both in my imprisonment and in the defense and confirmation of the gospel" (Phil. 1:7). That Paul would need and appreciate gifts of money under these circumstances is understandable, but this does not necessarily represent his general mode of operation.

Sometimes attention is drawn to the fact that when Paul was traveling in Greece, he was continually raising money from the churches there; this "collection" features prominently in his letters. While this is true, it is abundantly clear that none of this money was given for the use of Paul or his companions. The money was an offering from the Greek churches to "the poor among the saints at Jerusalem" (Rom. 15:26). It probably had a symbolic as well as practical meaning (Rom. 15:27). So eager was Paul to avoid any suggestion that these funds were being wrongly appropriated that he insisted that representatives from the churches concerned should bear the money in person to the Jerusalem church. Not only so, but these representatives were to be accredited by letter (1 Cor. 16:3). If the churches so desired, Paul would agree to travel with this group (1 Cor. 16:4). It is possible that the churches of Asia also participated in the project and that the list of persons named in Acts 20:4 is actually a record of the names of some of these delegates. In any event, Paul clearly dissociates himself from personal receipt of this money.

The Book of Acts, which records Paul's travels, indicates that Paul supported himself by practicing a trade. In his youth Paul was educated as a Pharisee, but he had also learned the skill of working with leather. In Corinth Paul sought out a Jewish couple who had recently emigrated from Italy. They welcomed Paul as a business partner, and he worked with them. Then on the Sabbath day Paul "argued in the synagogue," presenting the Christian message to both Jews and Greeks (Acts 18:1-4). This continued for a period of eighteen months (Acts 18:11). However, it was not in Corinth alone that Paul adopted such a practice. He lived in Ephesus for longer than two years. There his daily teaching sessions took place in "the hall of Tyrannus" (Acts 19:9), and some manuscripts read that he taught each day "from the fifth hour to the tenth," which would suggest that he utilized the siesta hours when it was too hot for active work. In his farewell address to the elders of the Ephesian church, Paul reminded them that in all the months he had ministered in Ephesus he had not needed to depend on others for material support: "I coveted no one's silver or gold or apparel. You yourselves know that these hands ministered to my necessities, and to those who were with me" (Acts 20:33-34). Paul's source of income was his own manual trade.

Paul consciously adopted a lifestyle that was in accord with the teaching of Jesus, and he did so in order to set an example for others: "In all things I have shown you that by so toiling one must help the weak, remembering the words of the Lord Jesus, how he said, 'It is more blessed to give than to receive'" (Acts 20:35). This lifestyle sometimes caused Paul privations: "I have learned the secret of facing plenty and hunger, abundance and want" (Phil. 4:12); "in toil and hardship, through many a sleepless night, in hunger and thirst, often without food, in cold and exposure" (2 Cor.

11:27). To Paul, these privations were nothing more than the necessary concomitants of the life to which he was called and which he had willingly embraced: "I do not account my life of any value nor as precious to myself, if only I may accomplish my course and the ministry which I received from the Lord Jesus" (Acts 20:24).

Did Paul assume that every Christian minister would live by the same principles? Not necessarily. After leaving Corinth, Paul found that he had to justify his position. Other Christian leaders did not work for a living in a secular sphere, and they did accept gifts of food and other things from Christian communities. Paul indicates that to accept such support would certainly be consistent with Jewish Law: "You shall not muzzle an ox when it is treading out the grain" (1 Cor. 9:9; Deut. 25:4). It would be consistent also with common practice: "Who serves as a soldier at his own expense? Who plants a vineyard without eating any of its fruit? Who tends a flock without getting some of the milk?" (1 Cor. 9:7). Certainly, Paul maintains, it is true that material gifts would be an appropriate expression of gratitude for spiritual service (1 Cor. 9:11). In fact, Paul recollects a command of Jesus to the effect that "those who proclaim the gospel should get their living by the gospel" (1 Cor. 9:14, probably a reference to Matt. 10:10). However, Paul reflects that he and Barnabas have chosen not to accept such gifts lest in so doing they give the impression that they are preaching to raise money for themselves rather than to impart something of value to their hearers. Consequently they are determined to "endure anything rather than put an obstacle in the way of the gospel of Christ" (1 Cor. 9:12). In so doing, Paul is well-aware that he is "not making full use of [his] right in the gospel" (1 Cor. 9:18). Nevertheless, he "would rather die" (1 Cor. 9:15) than change this practice for himself.

Two ideas emerge from this material. First, it was considered quite acceptable for Christian leaders to be paid for their ministry —although the provision of food and lodging seems to be indicated more clearly than actual gifts of money. And second, some early

Christian leaders saw good reasons for choosing not to accept any such remuneration. It is often thought that one standard applies to an itinerant ministry and the other to a more settled situation—that is, unlike the itinerant evangelist, the local pastor should receive a stipend. But this argument cannot be validly maintained in light of the fact that, over a span of twenty years or more, Paul's ministry was settled for several years at a time in particular places. And precisely when it was a settled ministry, Paul found occasion to work at a trade to earn a regular income.[1]

The early church found it necessary to guard against those who imagined that "godliness is a means of gain" (1 Tim. 6:5). Timothy was exhorted to ensure that a person selected for a church leadership position should be "no lover of money," "not greedy for gain" (1 Tim. 3:3, 8). The Didache indicates that the church was troubled by people who found that by posing as "prophets" or as "itinerant evangelists" they could prey on the hospitality of well-meaning Christians, enjoying the benefits of travel and sustenance without responsible commitment to work. Guidelines were drawn up to protect Christians from such people: "Let every apostle who comes to you be received as the Lord. But he shall not remain more than one day. But, if necessary, let him remain a second day. But, if he stays for three, he is a false prophet. And when the apostle departs, let him take only enough bread to last until he reaches shelter; but, if he asks for money, he is a false prophet" (Did. 11:4-6, in *FC,* 1:180). Christians were warned in the Didache that they should exercise wisdom in apportioning gifts. In a section which seems to depend heavily on the teaching of Jesus, the Didache reads: "Give to everyone who asks, and ask nothing in return. . . . But in this matter the saying also holds: 'Let your alms sweat in your hands until you know to whom you are giving'" (Did. 1:5-6, in *FC,* 1:172).

It was recognized very early in the Christian communities that gifts of money "in the name of the Lord" could actually have harmful effects if not given with discrimination.

Present-day Applications

How do these principles affect the church of today? They remind us that a church structure which depends on full-time paid ministry is not necessarily the ideal structure or the only viable option. There is certainly nothing sacred about it. If this structure has proved to be a satisfactory way of promoting the Christian faith in the world and of stimulating spiritual growth and development among Christians, then it should probably continue. But to determine its effectiveness, an honest appraisal of its strengths and weaknesses should be undertaken. Does this form of ministry call into question the motive behind a person's presentation of the gospel message? Does it encourage a spirit of competitiveness and self-aggrandizement? Does it provide an opportunity for unqualified and undisciplined people to "earn an easy living" at the expense of the Christian community?

A paid professional ministry supplies the church with leaders who are free to devote all of their energies to its organization and direction. In theory this sounds good. But a price has been paid beyond the mere outlay of money. Because the minister has been "paid to do the job," he or she is sometimes expected not simply to *lead* the church but to *be* the church. An artificial distinction has come about. The Christian leader is not viewed as *primus inter pares*, but as Christian par excellence. He or she is expected to embody all the virtues associated with the Christian experience and in this way to mediate Christ to the world. Once such a token Christian has been appointed, the larger community of Christians may feel that the responsibility has been lifted from its shoulders. The "average church member" is called by God to earn a living and to provide money with which a minister may be hired. The hired minister will then promote the cause of Christ and his kingdom.

Thus, it is not surprising that in the present-day church there is a strong feeling that the lay people have been overlooked and their gifts neglected. In many areas the desire is being expressed that the leadership skills of lay people should be developed and that opportunity should be given for these to be used. It is becoming recognized that leadership of a congregation calls for many and varied gifts and that not all of these are to be found in a particular minister. For the most part, these gifts are distributed among members of a congregation.

But if the minister is paid to lead the church, what right does he or she have to delegate to a member of the congregation leadership functions that are understood to be the minister's responsibility? Is not the person who works full-time in the secular world and who also leads a church activity giving more of himself or herself than the minister? And by what standard does one judge which church-related task receives payment and which may be assigned on a voluntary basis? Is there not some fallacy in a system in which, for example, a guest preacher may receive $100 for preaching a single sermon, while a Sunday school teacher may teach a class for fifty-two weeks in the year without receiving any financial remuneration whatsoever? And on what basis is it determined that a soloist making a musical presentation on one occasion deserves payment, while a choir member who faithfully participates in congregational worship fifty-two weeks of the year is considered a "volunteer"?

Given the average church situation, the paid minister is likely to cover tasks that command prestige and respect (such as preaching and leading worship), while unpaid members of the congregation will find themselves involved with tasks that command less prestige and respect (such as youth work, visitation, catering, and finances). Until recent times male members of our society were usually employed at a trade or business for a number of hours each day while female members were homemakers, so it was natural to turn to women when building up this unofficial task force. Married women were supported financially by their husbands and were, it was supposed, happy to have meaningful activities to supplement their routine home duties. Women thus developed various ministry skills but were not paid for their exercise. (It was this support network of women which made it possible for the male minister to run the church effectively.) Now that a large proportion of women work shoulder to shoulder with men in the secular world, the situation has changed somewhat. Often today both husband and wife are wage-earners and are working full-time. This unpaid work force is no longer available to the minister.

One way of responding to this situation is for a church to encourage and train lay people to give leadership in particular areas, sometimes paying them for this service. This response, however, may not be adequate, for as long as the church leader is paid a salary for his or her ministerial office, he or she is set apart from other church members. This is an artificial distinction. The New Testament indicates that spiritual gifts are distributed to all members of the Christian community and are intended to be used "for the common good" (1 Cor. 12:7). Gifts are not to lie dormant; they are to be used for the upbuilding of the entire community (Rom. 12:6-8; Eph. 4:11-16), and the worship assembly is one place where these varied gifts may be put into effect (1 Cor. 14:26-32). The gifts and abilities conferred by the Holy Spirit differ, but each gift has its own intrinsic value (1 Cor. 12:14-28). The church, however, has unduly elevated the gifts of preaching and teaching to positions of importance. When money is paid for these services but not for others, lesser value is attached to the exercise of the other spiritual gifts.[2]

Another way of responding to the present situation may be to suggest a move toward ministerial function of a voluntary nature, although the size of some churches and the enormous demands of ministry make this suggestion somewhat impractical. However, a number of other options are feasible. One might be to move in the direction of part-time ministerial appointments. Certain positive benefits could accrue from this. A minister who also works part-time in a secular field could bring to the ministerial function a realism which may otherwise be lacking. He or she could also have the opportunity of setting a practical example of how the Christian should operate in the secular community. This would command more respect than mere pulpit precept.

Of course it would be necessary to appoint more than one part-time minister to a congregation—perhaps three or four would be needed to replace each full-time minister. But this would not place a financial burden on the church if the main source of support for each is his or her own secular employment. It might involve the individual in some sacrifice of material comforts, but that would not be without biblical precedent. Of positive advantage to a church would be the fact that people of varied abilities would be ministering within the community. Rather than looking to one person for evidence of all the spiritual gifts, congregations could realistically assess the strengths of their members and encourage the diversity which they find among themselves. One person, for example, might have theological training and insight and would direct activities to promote spiritual growth; another might have the gift of evangelism and would assume responsibility for the church's outreach ministry; another might have particular aptitude for leading congregational worship, structuring it so that all may participate. This situation would permit more flexibility in the leadership function, with individuals serving in one capacity for several years and then yielding to others who are equally able. There may be times in an individual's life when he or she is more free or more able to exercise church leadership, and there may be other times when it would be advisable for the task to be yielded to others. The example of church leaders who are themselves prepared to sacrifice time and living standards to promote the message they proclaim may be all that is needed to encourage enthusiastic congregational participation in all of the other aspects of the church's life.

This suggestion may seem impractical or exceedingly difficult to implement. But it at least focuses attention on an issue that has sometimes been bypassed: There is no scriptural principle which requires that a church leader must be full-time in the service of the church, and there is no sacred edict which demands that the church leader must be paid for fulfilling such ministry. It is possible that the adoption of this form of leadership has led the church into the creation of an artificial distinction between leadership and laity, a distinction that has placed a heavy restraint on both. The leader has experienced the frustration of being expected to be competent in all areas of spiritual leadership, even though he or she may be gifted in only some of these areas; the laity has experienced the frustration of never having opportunity to develop the latent spiritual gifts which it senses in its midst. This has arrested the healthy growth and development of both.

Conclusions

The full-time paid ministry which has been accepted as the norm by many churches should not be regarded as the only or necessarily the best mode of directing a church's activities. Along with the positive contribution it has made to the church's life, there have been some negative influences. Not least of these is the tendency to view the minister as a token Christian, one who is expected to possess all the gifts of ministry. As a result, the minister finds himself or herself constantly working but never accomplishing the set goals because the goals themselves are unrealistic. In the past it was possible to find a partial solution to this problem. Women who were not employed outside the home were trained and deployed throughout the organizational structure of the church. They asked for and received no payment for their work. Now the social situation has changed. Many women who are raising children are also employed outside the home and have little free time available. The unpaid work force is diminished, but the task of ministry must continue, and women have a vital contribution to make. If full-time paid ministry is affirmed at the present time, then it is necessary to hire women in the same way that men have been hired in the past, on the basis of their call and their ability to serve. This will ensure the continued influence of women, even in view of the changing social structure. Only in this way will the church maintain a balanced ministry, with men and women working together in the exercise of spiritual gifts.

Notes

[1] It is strange that the Roman Catholic church, which has patterned its priesthood on the examples of Jesus and Paul in respect to celibacy, has ignored the example of Paul in respect to secular work. In both of these areas Paul claims to have adopted standards which differed from those of his peers.

[2] See E. Margaret Howe, "Women and Church Leadership," *Evangelical Quarterly* 51, no. 2 (April-June 1979): 97-104.

REFLECTIONS

THE CHURCH IS an ancient institution, and changes in its structure tend to come about slowly. At this present time, however, there is in many churches an openness to change and a desire to develop leadership models which will enhance the effectiveness of the Christian mission. There is a renewed interest in searching out the origins of Christian worship, and keen analysis is being made of the significance of historical development in the formation of church structure. Many churches have demonstrated a willingness to initiate change and to establish new organizational patterns. Reflection on some of the key issues may stimulate others to thought and action.

The Servant Model

The structure of the institutional church communicates a message to the world as surely as does its congregational worship, and that message ought to be consistent with the basic tenets of the Christian faith. The leadership model presented by Jesus to his disciples emphasized the significance of service. He discouraged the use of titles of honor and stressed the importance of humility: "The kings of the Gentiles exercise lordship over them; and those in authority over them are called benefactors. But not so with you; rather let the greatest among you become as the youngest, and the leader as one who serves" (Luke 22:25-26). This disposition was exemplified by Jesus as he led the community from which the church was born: "The Son of man also came not to be served but to serve" (Mark 10:45). The title "minister" (servant) is thus a natural title to use for a church leader. The sphere of ministerial service is threefold—the minister is a servant of God, a servant of other Christians, and a servant of men and women outside the Christian community. The New Testament documents present Jesus as one who "ministered" in all of these dimensions.

First, as a servant of God, the minister is required to maintain a lifestyle in accordance with God's design. The Hebrew psalmist expressed the sentiment in these words: "O Lord . . . who shall dwell on thy holy hill? He who walks blamelessly, and does what is right, and speaks truth from his heart" (Ps. 15:1-2). When Jesus assumed the form of a servant, his act entailed obedience to God (Phil. 2:6-8). The church leader must come to terms with the fact that servanthood demands allegiance and obedience to God. Next, as a servant of other Christians, the minister finds that his or her responsibilities are analogous to those of a parent. The minister is exhorted to provide the Christian community with spiritual sustenance (1 Peter 5:2), to guard the spiritual life of each member (Heb. 13:17), and to set an example of what it means to live as a Christian (1 Tim. 4:12). Finally, as a servant of men and women outside the Christian community, the minister must command respect (1 Tim. 3:7). He or she must have the ability to present the Christian faith in a reasonable manner and to handle the opinions of others with gentleness (2 Tim. 2:25).

In what sense does a minister serve a congregation? There are some who imagine that a minister must be ready to "fetch and carry" at all times for all people. Of course there will be times when the help of a minister is needed for unusually long and late hours, and to this extent a minister's schedule will often be unpredictable. But this is not all that is involved in service. Similar demands may be placed on a church secretary or a church janitor from time to time.

Servanthood may best be defined as a particular attitude with which the minister approaches his or her profession. Humility is a leadership virtue much praised in the Scriptures. A minister should cultivate an attitude of humility in relation to God and in relation to people. It is not enough for this to be assumed: it must be demonstrated.

Humility before God will be evident in the way a minister prays. Prayer is the warm expression of a growing and developing relationship between God and the one who prays. In audible prayer the minister reveals to others aspects of his or her own experience of God. This serves a double purpose—it presents the congregation with insight into a minister's true consciousness of the presence and person of God, and it serves as an example of personal communication with God which may be emulated by the congregation. The ministerial profession offers a natural outlet for prayer of this nature. Sessions of congregational worship usually allow time for prayer, and the prayers offered by the minister on such occasions reveal the minister's own spiritual depth. But perhaps more important are the times when the minister prays in less formal settings. Prayers offered in the presence of the church staff when church business is being conducted; prayers offered at mealtimes when the members of the church family eat together; prayers offered during counseling sessions or when the minister is visiting in the homes of members of the congregation—all of these reveal to others the attitude with which ministry is undertaken. As a child's attitude may be judged by the way in which the child addresses a parent, so a minister's attitude may be judged when the minister is "overheard" conversing with God.

Humility in relation to people will be evident in the way a minister conducts church affairs. An attitude of humility is sensed in the minister who permits members of a congregation to interact as equals and to serve the church with dignity. The minister who has cultivated this virtue will never trample people underfoot in order to achieve his or her goals or in order to ascend the hierarchical ladder. Humility precludes treating others as though their opinions are of little worth. Rather, the humble person is eager to hear the opinions of others and to integrate them into his or her own thinking. The humble person will give others credit for their insights and achievements and will not absorb the reflected glory as though it belonged to the leader alone.

A minister's attitudes surface readily and are usually noted by members of the congregation. They will elicit praise or censure, expressed or unexpressed. A minister's actions are weighed by observant onlookers, and as one who has accepted the role of being an example to others, a minister must not begrudge the fact that his or her life is carefully observed. A congregation which finances a full-time minister has the right to evaluate whether or not the minister is adequately fulfilling the assigned role. Certainly this is not to advocate constant personal appraisal and criticism, but it does draw attention to the fact that humility must be as much a way of life as it is a virtuous attitude. Humility is demonstrated in a personal lifestyle that is not ostentatious. A minister's dress, car, and home are significant indicators. A servant generally assumes a lifestyle somewhat less luxurious than that of those who are served. This would speak well in the affluent materialistic society of the Western world, but even more so in countries where there is greater material need. The minister needs balance and perspective in this area.

How can this servant model be reconciled with the biblical teaching that honor should be accorded spiritual leaders (1 Tim. 5:17)? Does this "honor" demand the "enthronement" of the minister, in the sense that he or she should be provided for lavishly? Unhappily, this has sometimes been the case. The higher a person ascends up the administrative hierarchy of the church, the more adulation that person receives—sometimes in the form of higher salaries and sometimes in the form of more lavish vestments and more elegant living accommodations. This is often justified by the argument that the living accommodations actually belong to the church, not to the individual. While this may be true, they nevertheless bestow social status and a living environment which is the envy of the majority of the working people of the world. Does this adequately portray the servant model? Certainly the Christian is exhorted to give "respect to whom respect is due" (Rom. 13:7), but has the church mistaken one form of respect for another?

How is the servanthood model affected by the hierarchical organization of many churches? A system in which appointments are made from the top of the hierarchy downward creates problems and is a cause of great unease. Instead of leaders being people of spiritual worth recognized and appointed by their peers, they are people who have been enabled to climb the ladder of promotion. Chance factors, such as those of race or sex, may feature heavily in promotion decisions. An elitist group may thus perpetuate itself by appointing to high positions only those who will ensure the continuance of the system unchanged, whether or not this system is adequately serving the needs of the church.

The servant model seems to be the dominant leadership model presented in the New Testament documents. But the spiritual leader is not without authority. In the tradition of the Hebrew prophets, the Christian leader is to "convince, rebuke, and exhort" (2 Tim. 4:2), and congregations are instructed to "obey [their] leaders and submit to them" (Heb. 13:17). How can such authority be exercised by one who is assuming the role of a servant? One might respond that such authority can be effectively exercised only by one who is assuming the role of a servant. When a congregation perceives in its minister a life of humble devotion to God and selfless commitment to people, then it will be ready to respond with respect and an attitude of obedience. But probably not until then.

Diversity in Ministry

Just as people differ from one another, so church structures differ from one another. It would be a mistake to insist on only one pattern of church leadership. Perhaps in the past churches have erred in this respect—they have allowed tradition to dictate the norm and have then resisted any deviation from this. The Roman Catholic church has limited itself to celibate male leadership; Protestant churches have largely limited themselves to married male leadership. Both are impoverished as a result. The early church evidently found richness in diversity, and the time has come for the present-day church to rediscover this wealth.

Christians meeting in community have many options in establishing leadership patterns. They may appoint one leader, who may be single or married, a man or a woman. Or they may choose to appoint a team of leaders, consisting of a husband and wife, or of an unrelated man and woman, or of two people of the same sex. The team may consist of co-leaders having equal responsibilities, or of a senior and junior partner. If necessity dictates, the team may consist of more than two members. The persons appointed to leadership may be salaried or unpaid. No matter what options are chosen, the leaders bring to the task of ministry those gifts with which they have been endowed by the Holy Spirit.

In the past, Protestant churches have strongly resisted the appointment of unmarried people as ministers. The situation is now changing. By placing single men and women in leadership positions, the Protestant church is once more affirming the value of celibacy. The church needs to recognize that the way of life chosen by these people should be openly held in honor, just as the married lifestyle has been honored in the past. Certainly sexual purity should be expected—fornication and adultery both fall short of the biblical ethical standard. But attitudes of suspicion directed toward single people should not be countenanced.

In the past, churches were strongly geared to the family unit. It was assumed that the majority of young people would marry and raise a family. But social structures are changing. Increasingly large numbers of people choose not to marry or not to raise a family. The church must therefore rethink its values and its strategy. The "singles' fellowship" no longer caters to a few people who happen not to be married. Its members are now found to be in the mainstream of the church's life. Divorced and widowed people are included in this group. Unmarried church leaders, therefore, serve as role models for a rising percentage of people in any church congregation. When the youth of the church are included in the assessment, it may be found that the single minister finds natural rapport with a larger section of the congregation than does the married minister.

As Protestant churches begin to appoint unmarried ministers, they should be careful not to overlook their special needs. In this respect much may be learned from the Roman Catholic tradition. The Roman Catholic church recognizes that a person who chooses a celibate lifestyle is particularly in need of a supportive community and a network of personal friendships. This is provided for such people. It may take the form of living accommodations shared by a small group of priests, with housekeeping duties provided at the expense of the church. Retreat centers around the country or overseas provide these church leaders with an environment in which they may relax and form new friendships. These are, of course, geared to the needs of single males. The Protestant church must provide realistically for the needs of both male and female single ministers. In addition, care should be taken to see that single ministers are not placed in isolated geographical areas. They do not take with them a supportive family unit, and they will find it difficult to develop friendships in such areas.

The possibilities of team ministry are also being widely recognized in churches across the United States. This is in itself a recognition of the value of diversity in leadership. Increasingly large numbers of married couples are entering the ministry as co-pastors and are working efficiently and effectively in local churches. Probably this represents the ideal of church leadership—with man and woman complementing one another in this role and thus more perfectly representing the image of God. It is not, of course, necessary for the team to be a married couple. It may be more convenient and less expensive if they are married, but there is no reason why a team might not consist of any two ordained persons. If men and women work side by side in business organizations, how much more should they be seen working side by side in the church! The fear expressed by some is more an admission of weakness or of jealousy than it is a rational objection to the principle. If a man and a woman cannot work side by side in a church leadership context without unlawful indulgence of passion, where can they work side by side? The church leadership situation directs attention toward a wide variety of people and of activities—a situation that may be most effectively met by diversity in the leaders.

Spiritual Gifts and Seminary Training

The New Testament indicates clearly that every Christian is endowed by the Holy Spirit with particular spiritual gifts. These are diverse in nature, but all have a common goal—to edify or build up the body of Christ, the church. Some of these gifts equip a person for leadership positions: Paul states that God has placed within the church such people as apostles, prophets, and teachers (1 Cor. 12:28). Members of the church in Rome were encouraged to put these gifts to use, not let them lie dormant (Rom. 12:6-8). Timothy, a young church leader in Ephesus, was exhorted not to neglect his spiritual gifts, but to develop them (1 Tim. 4:14-15). In practical terms, church congregations have a role to play in identifying spiritual gifts and in encouraging their development. This is particularly true when leadership gifts are under consideration. Discernment is necessary in this area.

Characteristically, Protestant churches have identified the gift of preaching as being a most significant gift. But not everyone who has the ability to stand up and address a group of people is called to be a preacher. In pioneer days when the preaching was often conducted out-of-doors and before large crowds of people, it was necessary for the preacher to have a loud voice and decisive gestures in order to communicate the message. Even today there are people who assess a person's "call to ministry" by such criteria. The significant issue, however, is not the manner in which the communication takes place but the content of the message communicated. Church members are edified only insofar as the message communicated rightly represents the mind of God as expressed in Scripture. Certainly the preacher must also have the ability to express ideas in a clear and intelligible manner, but that in itself is not enough. Common experience over many years has been that church leadership is a calling which requires a multiplicity of skills. Some of these may be natural abilities; some may be abilities which surface when a person becomes a Christian; and some may be acquired only through long hours of study, training, or experience.

Of these skills, one of the most important is a knowledge of the Scriptures and an ability to interpret these in a meaningful way. Training in biblical exegesis, therefore, will always be an important part of the seminary program. It is essential that church leaders should have the ability of "rightly handling the word of truth" (2 Tim. 2:15). In this respect, above all others, congregations need able leadership.

There is, however, a sense in which biblical exegesis is a means to an end. An objective understanding of scriptural teachings is a matter of the mind only. An effective church leader moves the congregation from mental assent to practical application. The Christian faith demands both understanding and action. The minister must be able to so apply the biblical message that it results in changed attitudes and lives. He or she must be trained to be alert to the everyday life situation of a congregation—its needs, its joys, its problems, its choices, its challenges. If the Christian faith has meaning at all, it is to be found in the ebb and flow of family life and factory life and professional life; in the next-door neighbor who stands in need of the redemptive act of God, for it is before that neighbor that the Christian life is lived. What principles govern the normative life of the Christian, and what spiritual energies are available to aid in the application of these principles? Unless exegetical exposition of Scripture is accompanied by practical application, it may be empty and ineffective.

But the church leader is required to do more than preach to the non-Christian and teach the Christian. The way many churches are organized, the minister must also exercise professional business skills. The minister must make decisions concerning finances—such as the purchase of church property and equipment and the placing of investments. The minister must delegate responsibilities for the daily running of the church, secretarial duties, program planning, and the operation of committees. Behind the so-called "spiritual ministry" of the church is an organizational structure that can only operate effectively with the exercise of administrative skills. It is naïve to assume that a minister is responsible only for "spiritual leadership"; most will find themselves committed to much more than this.

Professional ministry requires wide-ranging knowledge and ability. To what extent is the seminary preparing men and women for such professional performance? Many seminarians have found that their training gave them a love for ancient languages and an ability to handle library research projects but did not equip them for the "real-life" situations encountered in churches. The seminary classroom readily addresses homiletical problems and the mechanics of preaching, but the psychology of interpersonal relationships and methods of handling conflict must often be figured out later by the minister when he or she is alone and in a field situation. Some seminarians find that the seminary is silent on current social and personal issues—issues that are prominent in the churches to which they are appointed. Such matters as how to handle interracial problems within a congregation, how to counsel effectively when faced with a wide spectrum of problems relating to sexuality, and how to deal with inner conflicts and tensions were never touched on during the years of seminary training. Some argue that the task of the seminary is to give a broad-based educational foundation on which the seminarian may build when appointed to a church and faced with practical situations. Others respond that no other sphere of professional training would be so narrowly defined. Do medical doctors learn only chemistry and biology, or do they learn also how to treat patients? These are issues with which seminaries must grapple.

An alternative response is to face realistically the possibility of more specialization in the field of ministry. To some extent this has taken place over the years with churches appointing a minister of education, a minister of music, a minister of youth, and a minister of recreation in addition to the position of senior minister. There is, however, another possibility for the division of duties. Perhaps it is too much to expect any one person to acquire all of the skills presently required of a minister. Instead, church leaders might become specialists in a particular area and might serve a number of churches in this one capacity. For example, one person might serve as theologian, one as business administrator, one as counselor, and one as evangelist. In this way each would contribute only those skills or abilities in which he or she excels.

This specialization would be a more realistic reflection of the New Testament teaching that spiritual gifts are distributed widely among Christians. In fact, Scripture teaches that no one Christian may claim that he or she possesses all of the leadership gifts (1 Cor. 12:28-30). The effect of this individual "incompleteness" is to draw the church together for mutual sharing of abilities and thus to create healthy interdependence. A sharing of the leadership function in any given church would create a model for each member of the church body to emulate. It would help to protect the church from the polarization of "priest" and "laity," of "minister" and "congregation." It would enable Christians to understand more clearly that they are the body of Christ and that the leader they appoint is simply one who serves them.

CONCLUSION

This book has addressed issues relating to women and church leadership. A study of Jewish and early Christian models has been made in an attempt to trace the reasons why women have for centuries been excluded from positions of prestige and influence in the church. In identifying these reasons, discussion has ranged over the development of the concept of the church leader as a priest, the gradual introduction of rules requiring church leaders to be celibate, and the widespread practice of appointing a full-time paid minister to a church. It has been shown that once this pattern was established, it became self-perpetuating, and women were excluded from leadership on the basis of longstanding tradition.

That this is not the only viable model of church leadership has been established by redirecting attention to Scripture and by identifying the subtle and sometimes unwholesome influences which fashioned the course of history. Recommendations have been made not only for the inclusion of women in professional church ministry but also for more far-reaching changes in the patterns of church leadership. Here the author's task is finished and the reader's task begins.

APPENDIX A

QUESTIONNAIRE FOR WOMEN SEMINARIANS

Name of seminary _____ Year of study _____
State _____

Are you intending to enter some form of Christian ministry?
Yes _____ No _____ If "yes," please indicate your area of interest (education, music, pastor, etc.).

Christians sometimes suggest that a person is "called by God" to fulfill church leadership roles. Do you consider you have been so "called"?
Yes _____ No _____ Possibly _____ If affirmative, describe the influences, events, experiences, etc., which have helped or are helping you to identify this call.

What special aptitudes do you have which would enable you to function well in a leadership role?

Have you ever had any misgivings about your "call" to ministry?
Yes _____ No _____ If "yes," please describe them.

What encouragement have you had from (a) your home church, (b) friends, (c) seminary faculty?

In your seminary, what is the approximate number of:
teachers: male _____ female _____
students: male _____ female _____

Have you encountered any specific problems in seminary (related to theological issues, practical issues, classroom situations, etc.) which you attribute to the fact that you are a woman? If so, please describe them and suggest any solutions you may have found.

Can you suggest any ways in which your seminary could more effectively train women for ministry?

Would you encourage other women to pursue seminary training and enter full-time Christian ministry? Yes _____ No _____ If "no," why not? If "yes," what advice would you give them?

Are you satisfied with the present concept of church leadership, or are there changes you would like to see?

Have you ever heard an ordained woman preach? Yes _____ No _____ If "yes," what was your reaction to this experience?

Are you in favor of the ordination of women? Yes _____ No _____ Please give careful reasons for your response.

Is it your desire to receive ordination? Yes _____ No _____ Possibly _____ If affirmative, do you forsee any problems finding a full-time appointment, considering the fact that you are a woman? How would you react to these problems if such did arise?

What do you think is an appropriate mode of dress for a woman leading congregational worship?

In view of the mixed climate of opinion over the ordination of women, what special qualities do you feel a woman should have if she is to succeed in this field?

Have you ever had any church-related experiences where a problem has arisen because you are a woman? Yes _____ No _____ If "yes," please describe them.

Are there any aspects of church leadership which you feel a man can handle better than a woman?

Are there any aspects of church leadership you feel a woman can handle better than a man?

What significance do you attach to a ceremony of ordination as performed in your particular church?

Please add any further comments relating to women and ministry.

APPENDIX B

QUESTIONNAIRE FOR WOMEN MINISTERS

TRAINING AND PLACEMENT

Where did you receive your academic and/or professional training?

How many women teachers did you have, and in what area did they teach?

How many years were you in training? What qualifications do you hold?

What professional positions have you held?

How did you obtain these?

Did you at any time encounter problems obtaining employment on account of the fact that you are a woman? If so, please describe them.

PRESENT APPOINTMENT

Denomination _____ _ City _____ State _

Title of position _____ Married _____ Single _____

Duties and responsibilities _ _____

_____

How long have you been employed in this position? _____

Do you work alone? _____ With colleagues? _____ (male) _____

(female) _____ If you work with colleagues, what positions do they hold?

CALL TO MINISTRY

What factors or circumstances convinced you of your "call" to ministry?

What kind of advice did you receive and from whom?

Have you at any time had inner doubts about this call? If so, for what reasons?

Can you identify any people who were your "role models"? (I do not need names—just who these people were.)

PROBLEM AREAS

It is known that some women ministers have had problems in some of these areas. If sections do not apply to you, please pass. If sections do apply to you, please describe particular incidents (no names necessary). I am specifically concerned with problems arising from the fact that you are a *woman* minister. I would value also indications of any *solutions* you may have found.

Areas of ministry you are not permitted to participate in.

Salary differences between you and male colleagues performing similar professional duties.

Personal relationships with male colleagues.

Relationships with other members of the church staff (secretaries, etc.).

Response from the congregation.

Inner doubts, uncertainties, fears?

Any other problem area?

What is the biggest problem women ministers face?

SUGGESTIONS

Are there any areas in which you feel that *seminaries* could better prepare women for ministry?

Some *congregations* are reluctant to appoint women as ministers. Can you suggest ways to help overcome this attitude?

What do you think is an appropriate mode of *dress* for a woman leading congregational worship?

In which *areas of ministry,* if any, do you think that women might be more effective than men and vice versa?

In view of the present mixed climate of opinion, what special *qualities* do you think a woman minister needs?

What *advice* would you give to a young woman considering whether to train as a minister?

Are you satisfied with the present *concept* of church leadership, or are there changes you would like to see?

GENERAL INDEX

Abbesses, 39

American Baptist Church, 139–142

American Lutheran church; Lutheran Church in America; and Lutheran Church—Missouri Synod, 121, 148–153, 187, 190, 208

Apostle, 16, 24, 27, 35, 42n10, 68, 69, 70, 71–73, 91, 135, 136

Assemblies of God, 138–139

Bible
interpretations, 15–27
study, 10–11
translation, 29–32, 42

Bishop, 36, 38, 39, 69, 70, 72–77, 92

Call to ministry, 162–168

Canonesses, 39

Celibacy, 105–128

Christian Church (Disciples of Christ), 146–148

Church secretary, 24

Church soloist, 26

Coptic church, 131

Deacon, 16, 30–34, 36, 69, 70, 77–81, 92, 122, 123, 131

Divorce, 107

Eastern Orthodox church, 94, 95, 121–122, 124, 130–132, 159n1–7

Elder (presbyter), 16, 68, 69, 73–77, 92

Episcopal church, 208

Eucharist, 93, 97, 98, 101, 102, 133

Evangelist, 16, 27

Head covering, 21, 58, 59–61

High priest, 91

Lutheran Church in America, *See* American Lutheran Church

Lutheran Church—Missouri Synod, *See* American Lutheran Church

Marriage (mutual submission), 54–58

Mennonite church, 186

Money (salary for ministers), 23, 210, 213–226, 230

Ordination, 27, 58, 94, 95, 96, 99, 129–160

Orthodox church, 159n1–7

Passover, 19

Pharisees, 88

Presbyterian Church, U.S., 157–158

Priest, 23, 83–104, 122

Prophet, 16, 58, 61, 68, 69, 70–71, 84–85, 87

Protestant churches, 124–126, 138–158, 232, 233, 234

INDEX OF PERSONS

INDEX OF BIBLICAL REFERENCES